The Sadness Will Last Forever

A Tribute to Vincent van Gogh

SUMIT DUTTA

Dedicated to

Suparna, Priya and Sourojit

Vincent van Gogh - Charcoal Drawing

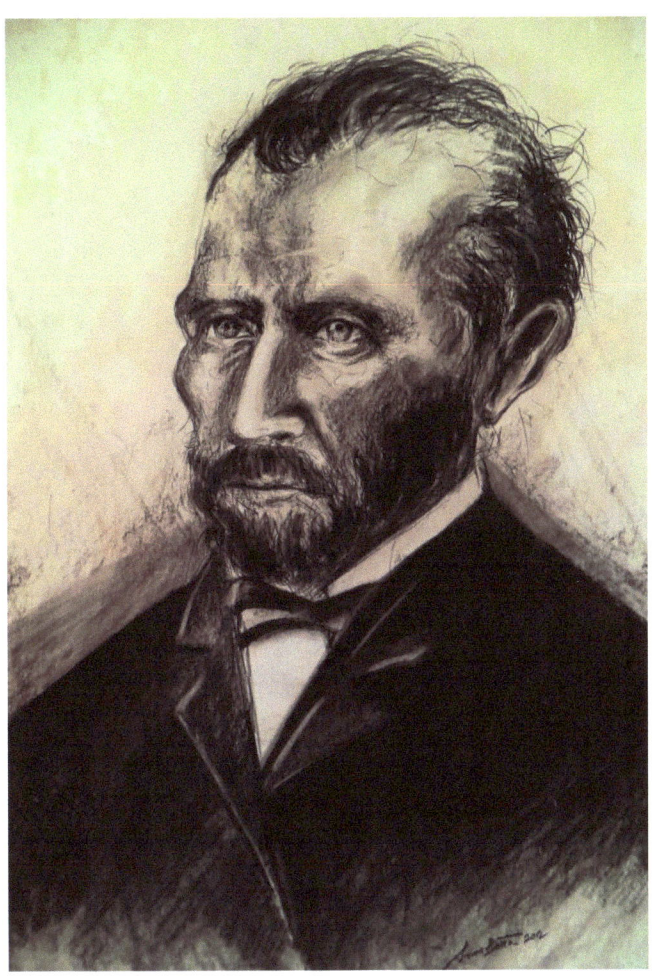

Table of Contents

Prelude 9

Artists are Exceptionally Emotional Creatures 11

Nature is The Master 12

Healing Effect of Art – Artists as Healers 15

Essence of Van Gogh's Experiment 18

Artists and Their Audiences and the Middle Man 22

True Artists are Embodiment of True Spirituality 25

Plato's Philosopher King and Van Gogh's Pure Spiritual Aesthetics 28

"Passion of Vincent" – A New Experimental Painting Media 30

Why "The Sadness Will Last Forever?" 34

The "Madness" Will Last Forever 38

"Passion of Vincent" – Paintings 40

Prelude

"The sadness will last forever" – these were reportedly the last words uttered by Vincent van Gogh to his brother Theo. And throughout my journey to learn painting I am searching the meaning of these words. Let me clearly state at the beginning of this book that this is not a book on life and biography of Vincent van Gogh, rather it is an enquiry and an effort to understand and touch the depth of his artistic passions. My readings of Van Gogh and study of his art works are permeated by deep emotion which I felt when I have gone through them. And I must confess that the long diligent and intelligent readings of Van Gogh's life and works did not take me to anywhere rather than to have some bizarre conclusions and fragmented comprehensions. Instead one day, may be serendipitously, just when I started to work with bold brush strokes and use colors like a mad man I started to find some of the hidden meanings of Van Gogh's works. Yes, that time I was deviating from the traditional techniques. I was just destroying so many canvases and surfaces yet I was becoming restless. I wanted to paint like Van Gogh. Again I was studying his paintings but this time with a different eye and mind set. And I just heard an inner voice – do not look at them with your eyes, feel them with your soul. And yes this time I was astonished to discover that his paintings are so childish yet so artistic. These two seemingly opposite characteristics make Van Gogh different from others. In most of his landscapes we find as if a playful child is playing with colors on the canvases in the lap of nature. It looked so easy yet it was so difficult to reproduce that. And this was the time I was convincing myself that I will go deeper and deeper in to the ocean of aesthetics created by Van Gogh. I worked day and night to search for a media by which I can paint like Van Gogh. And one day I found something which seems to be really childish yet artistic and I call this Media "Passion of Vincent".

Nobody in this world cares for such experiments. It is a diligent and super intelligent world out there. It is just a mega market place and whichever sells in the market will have value.

We know Van Gogh's paintings did not sell in the market so the man had to suffer failures after failures.

He was sad, he suffered depression yet no artist or so called art critics were there to feel him. Yes I emphasize the word feel him. And that is why he was sad and the sadness lasted throughout his artistic career. And that sadness never ends for those who want to paint like him and follow his path. This book is an enquiry why 'the sadness will last forever'. And to share some of my works painted in the newly discovered media by me 'Passion of Vincent' as a tribute to the great soul.

Artists are Exceptionally Emotional Creatures

Van Gogh said "A great fire burns with in me, but no one stops to warm themselves at it and passers – by only see a wisp of smoke". This may be starting point of the suffering of an artist. Artists are born with some fire with in. The nature of this fire may be a subject of debate but according to me this fire is the essence of artistic potential of an artist. While others love nature and beautiful things in the nature artists want to preserve, recreate and reflect upon that. While others can see the things artists can feel them through eyes. An artistic mind finds movements in air, water, fire and earth and can feel the life in even the nonliving things. Artists can understand the language of light and the grammar of shadows. For an artist all the creatures have specific energy and language hidden in its appearance. This subliminal language, unheard sound, unspoken words of the natural things burns as a fire inside an artist. This peculiar fire makes artists exceptionally emotional creatures.

Why do artists suffer? They internally burn due to the heat of this fire. And also they burn because it is difficult to communicate about this fire to others. Artists have to find newer techniques, unique experiments and innovative media to convince and communicate with others. Yet there is no certainty that the artist will succeed. In fact most of the radical artistic experiments end up in failures. That is why Van Gogh says "no one stops to warm themselves at it". For an extraordinary artistic soul like Van Gogh there can be some point of time where the human soul and the natural beauty mingles with each other in an inseparable way and that is the time of flow of streams of passion. In such flow of impulsive passion the artist utters such words like "The sunflower is mine, in a way". The common person perceives it as madness but in fact it is the flow of love, endless love of an artistic heart. "It is good to love many things, for therein lies the true strength, and whosoever loves much performs much, and can accomplish much and what is done in love is well done" were the words of Van Gogh which brings us to the conclusion that such artistic souls are always in love with many things. And we can be sure of this insane love when we hear from him "If you truly love nature, you will find beauty everywhere." But why artists love nature so intensely. Yet again there may be controversies but according to me artists are conscious that they are nothing but a part of nature. So in that sense artistic love of nature can be considered as a kind of self-love.

Nature is The Master

"We are surrounded by poetry on all sides" says Van Gogh as he goes on to paint great number of landscapes on his canvases. And truly most of the great masters have reiterated that nature is the master for many a time in the history of art. But I think there is confusion in this area. Even if we are painting a flower vase or making a portrait indoors we are copying the things in the nature. So it can be considered logically that all the things however artificial it may be are part of nature. Then the question comes what the masters try to really mean by the words nature is the master. Let us go in some more depth in to it and look for what Van Gogh had to say. Here are some thoughts of Van Gogh which may help us to understand the deeper meaning hidden in this notion.

….."At present I absolutely want to paint a starry sky. It often seems to me that night is still more richly coloured than the day; having hues of the most intense violets, blues and greens. If only you pay attention to it you will see that certain stars are lemon-yellow, others pink or a green, blue and forget-me-not brilliance. And without my expatiating on this theme it is obvious that putting little white dots on the blue-black is not enough to paint a starry sky."…….

……"If one feels the need of something grand, something infinite, something that makes one feel aware of God, one need not go far to find it. I think that I see something deeper, more infinite, more eternal than the ocean in the expression of the eyes of a little baby when it wakes in the morning and coos or laughs because it sees the sun shining on its cradle."……

……"If you truly love nature, you will find beauty everywhere"…..

If we just analyze the above thoughts we will get a nice idea about the deeper meaning of the notion - nature is the master. It is not the color we see of the natural things which must guide us to use our paints but the feeling it generates within us must guide us to use our paints. There can be two extremes of the subject matter choice in art. One extreme is total formlessness and absolute abstraction and the other extreme is absolute detailing and realistic depiction of things.

The problem of both these contents is that it produces monotony and boredom for the artist. And frankly speaking for both the extremes we can use artificial intelligence and digital technology to produce them in innumerable numbers. For both these extremes what we need is lots of intelligence and artistic skills and techniques. Yet that have its own limitation because things produced by intelligence have appeal mainly to intelligence.

Let us consider the other side where the subject matter remains constant but the way the artists see it or rather feel it differs. And that is more emotional than intelligent in nature. It sounds odd when Van Gogh says "It often seems to me that night is still more richly coloured than the day" to an intelligent ear but for an emotional ear it is just a piece of poetry. The artistic feeling of Van Gogh is finding "hues of the most intense violets, blues and greens". How many among us have really seen or rather felt "that certain stars are lemon-yellow, others pink or a green, blue"? And not only that, they have their own "brilliance" too. And this depth of fathomless feelings led Van Gogh to conclude "putting little white dots on the blue-black is not enough to paint a starry sky" and that is why we find a lot of hallow and vibrant colors around Van Gogh's stars.

And yes this deep analysis of his thoughts takes our perceptions about art to a new height. Van Gogh can see or rather feel infiniteness even in small things. This color of mind and the imaginative power can lead one to conclude that "If one feels the need of something grand, something infinite, something that makes one feel aware of God, one need not go far to find it." Yes these words sounds like a spiritual teacher is reflecting upon deep philosophical aspects of life and existence. In all objects the artistic eye can find aesthetic dimensions. It may be rock, mountain, a hay stack, river, an old tea pot or a hen or a piece of stone, a meadow or a willow tree. Feeling the divine beauty in common and ordinary things, finding limitlessness with in a limit, finding light in darkness, darkness in light is the purpose of study in art. Otherwise art will just reduce to some pigments, techniques and step wise demonstrations of those techniques.

To put this subjective perspective is the uniqueness of fine arts and painting. High resolution cameras can objectively capture the flawless detailing of anything but it is the human mind and its affective domain which can modulate the colors accordingly and change the perspective.

It is only the artistic works and its imaginative perspectives which can communicate the message that there may be infinite numbers between any two numbers and we must not be very serious about objectivity.

So when Van Gogh can "see something deeper, more infinite, more eternal than the ocean in the expression of the eyes of a little baby when it wakes in the morning and coos or laughs because it sees the sun shining on its cradle" it is just that infiniteness he is beholding in the eyes of that little baby. And therefore he goes on to say that "If you truly love nature, you will find beauty everywhere."

Healing Effect of Art – Artists as Healers

According to Van Gogh "Art is to console those who are broken by life." And that is in short the essence of all that any form of fine arts has to offer to humanity. Pain and suffering is an integral part of life. Life and death are the two aspects of the existence of any species on earth and humans are not an exception. Society and social institutions and transactions are nothing but a byproduct of human experiments to survive on earth. But there is a fundamental difference between all other social institution and art particularly fine arts. All our social institutions like state, marriage, education, family, justice system all have predominantly utilitarian value while fine arts is having predominantly spiritual value. Classical music compositions, a piece of painting, sculpture, a lyrical ballad all have just spiritual value nothing else. And the ultimate use of such a thing is to "console those who are broken by life." So art is in the deep analysis an entity which has tremendous healing power. In that sense artists are a form of healers. But do we feel in that way? Does the society feel and visualize artists in that way? Do the artistic experiments get proper familial, social and state support? No, often not. And that is the starting point of suffering for the artist.

Here is an account of how Van Gogh suffered in his own words "What am I in the eyes of most people — a nonentity, an eccentric, or an unpleasant person — somebody who has no position in society and will never have; in short, the lowest of the low. All right, then — even if that were absolutely true, then I should one day like to show by my work what such an eccentric, such a nobody, has in his heart. That is my ambition, based less on resentment than on love in spite of everything, based more on a feeling of serenity than on passion. Though I am often in the depths of misery, there is still calmness, pure harmony and music inside me. I see paintings or drawings in the poorest cottages, in the dirtiest corners. And my mind is driven towards these things with an irresistible momentum."

This is just a heart breaking account of how society usually reacts to the novel artistic innovations and experiments. How the society makes an artist feel that he is just a non-entity and an eccentric personality.

And this can be taken as a typical example of the contradiction between a true artist and the society and societal norms. Van Gogh can "see paintings or drawings in the poorest cottages, in the dirtiest corners" because he is a healer who wants to create art which can "console those who are broken by life" yet the society or the art critics are not matured enough to understand that.

How the wealth - hungry art critic will understand the artistic healing power of a sketch and drawing of a farmer or a sewage worker or the countryside damsel? They are more concerned with just the material value of the paintings to be displayed in the big art galleries where shallow minded art dealer will deal with even shallower minded art buyer and they will write the account of that transaction for their next pay off. They can only understand this when the person becomes famous somehow in spite of their full non-cooperation and resistance.

Does a true artist want to be famous? The answer is both yes and no. Yes, because the artist wants to deal with his viewers with his healing power and see how his art can really "console those who are broken by life." No, because artist does not want the popularity and glamour like what happens for all other common place craftsman. And here is what Van Gogh tells us in this matter "I want to touch people with my art. I want them to say 'he feels deeply, he feels tenderly'." All artists who have a great soul like Van Gogh want to find out this healing touch. And is that an easy job? No not at all; In fact it is the most difficult task in the world. To touch somebody's heart by few brush strokes is a job of paramount difficulty.

 The whole process is so hard that at the end the artist becomes a patient and most of the cases he finds no one to console when he himself gets broken by life. At some point he starts to think like Van Gogh "I wish they would take me as I am." Or "I'm such a nobody." Or "To suffer without complaint is the only lesson we have to learn in this life." And yes that is the ultimate lesson an artist learns from his whole artistic journey. His heart will burn, his mind will be torn apart, he will be deserted by everybody, nobody will take him as he is, every now and then he will feel that he is a just a simple nobody but he must absorb each and every thing and silently bear all the pain and suffering. While the physicians are the healers of physical health of the people, the artists are the spiritual healers for them.

They must go on accomplishing that great duty even if they themselves become broken by life. Whatever mental illness the doctors might have diagnosed for Van Gogh is a matter of research and controversy but I feel very strongly that Van Gogh was suffering from this situation which every divine innovator had to face from the society from time immemorial. May it be the pre historic cave painters or the renaissance painters all had to go through the same eternal suffering path way to attain the immortal artist - hood.

And when it comes to touch the people or to console them the technique matters a lot. Art becomes a product because of the monotony and repetitions of the technique or the subject matter. So it is the divine duty of the artist to break this monotony. All the great artists get restless to break the shackles of repetitive techniques. As we hear from Van Gogh "I would rather die of passion than of boredom." When the two century long established techniques were selling in the market place then Van Gogh was screaming inside his mind "Normality is a paved road: It's comfortable to walk, but no flowers grow on it." When an inner voice calls the artist that there is a need to change the artist just become insanely passionate about that change. Because he can feel that the current art is just selling in the market and it has lost its healing power. Van Gogh felt it and embarked in a dangerous sea of uncertainty.

Essence of Van Gogh's Experiment

This is not a traditional and academic analysis about the technique of Van Gogh. Readers can refer innumerable books and articles written on Post – Impressionism and its evolution in the historical context. It is just the expression of the feelings what I gathered after staring at the paintings of Van Gogh for years and years all together. It would be quite absurd to say that Van Gogh unknowingly or unconsciously did the experiments what he did, rather it is very evident from the analysis of his thoughts that he knew what he was doing is very innovative, novel yet dangerous. He clearly stated that "The fishermen know that the sea is dangerous and the storm terrible, but they have never found these dangers sufficient reason for remaining ashore." Following quotations will help us understand what Van Gogh was actually doing during his artistic experimentations:

….."What would life be if we had no courage to attempt anything?"……
….."I try more and more to be myself, caring relatively little whether people approve or disapprove."……
….."I am always doing what I cannot do yet, in order to learn how to do it."…..
….."Let us keep courage and try to be patient and gentle. And let us not mind being eccentric, and make distinction between good and evil."…..
….."I shouldn't precisely have chosen madness if there had been any choice, but once such a thing has taken hold of you, you can't very well get out of it."…..
….."I long so much to make beautiful things. But beautiful things require effort and disappointment and perseverance."…..
….."If I cease searching, then, woe is me, I am lost. That is how I look at it - keep going, keep going come what may."…..

….."How difficult it is to be simple!"……

….."If you work with love and intelligence, you develop a kind of armour against people's opinions, just because of the sincerity of your love for nature and art. Nature is also severe and, to put it that way, hard, but never deceives and always helps you to move forward."……

……"Many people seem to think it foolish, even superstitious, to believe that the world could still change for the better. And it is true that in winter it is sometimes so bitingly cold that one is tempted to say, 'What do I care if there is a summer; its warmth is no help to me now.' Yes, evil often seems to surpass good. But then, in spite of us, and without our permission, there comes at last an end to the bitter frosts. One morning the wind turns, and there is a thaw. And so I must still have hope."……

A deep analysis of the above mentioned thoughts of Van Gogh can help us to reach about the essence of his artistic experiment. What I perceive about his experiments and so called eccentricity is that he was choosing this eccentricity and insanity very consciously. But why? During his time due to the monotony of the tones and repetitive techniques art was losing its healing power or the spiritual power. This kind of thing happened many a times in the history of art.

Use of limited number of colors and established techniques had made paintings predictable. Somewhere deep inside his heart Van Gogh felt that agony and decided to break it. He knew that he had almost an impossible task ahead of him and may be at the very beginning he would have thought how dangerous it would have been to embark on that. He is going to break royal walls of established, frozen and ossified traditions without any prior experience. That is why he is identifying himself with the fishermen who "know that the sea is dangerous and the storm terrible." Was Van Gogh conscious of this danger or did he have the assessment of the extent of the whole adventure? Yes of course. He assessed this venture as that of "choosing madness" but he was in complete identification with this madness as he confessed that "once such a thing has taken hold of you, you can't very well get out of it." Was it a spell? Was it some uncanny energy that got hold of Van Gogh's consciousness? No, in my opinion it is the undying spirit of the pre - historic painters which got hold of Van Gogh's soul.

This undying spirit creates havocs when they enter an artist's soul. The artist gets tormented, depressed, and insane yet the true artist never wants to come out of it. This is the pristine spirit of expressing the emotions and sentiments.

This spirit is the edifice on which all the dimensions of human aesthetics stand. This spirit of self-expression is transcendent and keeps the wheel of art rolling.

This is ceaseless and deathless energy which keeps the artistic passions alive on earth.

Van Gogh was by choice becoming eccentric as he clearly states "Let us keep courage and try to be patient and gentle. And let us not mind being eccentric, and make distinction between good and evil." He knew very well that eccentricity is the best way to be productive and creative and that is why he consciously became eccentric at the cost of producing both good and evil. He knew that after the eccentric spell gets over he could sort out goods and evils.

While many experts identify many of Van Gogh's behavior as extreme madness I think most of them are part of his conscious eccentric adventure. If we do not understand this we may commit a very big mistake to evaluate the artistic contributions of this great soul. Precisely it was this eccentric adventure which led Van Gogh to endlessly search for newer and newer technique when he says "If I cease searching, then, woe is me, I am lost. That is how I look at it - keep going, keep going come what may." In the process of intense search of newer techniques Van Gogh was ready to ignore the public opinion on him as he declares "I try more and more to be myself, caring relatively little whether people approve or disapprove." Most of his techniques were disapproved that time by the people yet he never minded all these and moved on.

That is pure artistic consciousness. Knowing fully well that the public opinion was adverse he went on to work on with his own eccentric adventures. This conscious battle of Van Gogh against the prevailing public opinion is evident in the following words "If you work with love and intelligence, you develop a kind of armour against people's opinions, just because of the sincerity of your love for nature and art. Nature is also severe and, to put it that way, hard, but never deceives and always helps you to move forward." And this genuine artistic consciousness keeps the artistic imaginative and innovative power alive as he advises others to be innovative in the following message "do not become the slave of your model".

The search and the thirst for newer innovation and creative potential becomes such that the inner soul of Van Gogh screams from within that "The only time I feel alive is when I'm painting." That is the whole existence of a person has completely mingled with its purpose. And the purpose was to put some spiritual color to art, to reestablish the spiritual healing power of art. And Van Gogh thought that the best way he can do it is by breaking the established rules and making it simple. To find out the simplest way to capture light, depict movements and reflections and shadows. But that was not simple.

The revolutionary mind of Van Gogh made an open rebellion against the established rules yet stumbled upon the hurdles of techniques; the techniques to make things simple. It was difficult and really difficult to make things simple and Van Gogh astonishingly found that "How difficult it is to be simple!" Yet he never turned back from this most difficult task in the earth to be simple and experimented till the last day of his life because as a true artistic soul he knew "What would life be if we had no courage to attempt anything?" This is according to me the essence of the revolution called Vincent Van Gogh. In its core there is a conscious effort to set a dangerous destiny, put the whole heart and soul to accomplish the tasks and at last just to live for that. We are not just indebted to Van Gogh for his innovations and techniques we are also indebted to him for this lesson which he taught us by living every moment for the cause to up hold the spiritual ideals of art.

Artists and Their Audiences and the Middle Man

Throughout the history of art we have found a serious problem where there is an obstacle for the artists to communicate with their targeted audiences directly. There is a section of opportunistic parasite, the middle man between the artist and its audience. The essence of functioning of this middle man group is to create a peculiar aura and hallow around the established and famous artists and to get benefited materially by selling the aura. For their smooth functioning this middle man group domesticates another group called the art critics and art analyzers. Most of the cases these art critics are failed entrepreneurs in almost all endeavors in life, unskilled and ill-informed in any human knowledge domain. The only quality these people have is that they are utterly dogmatic and filled with some selected vocabulary to frame sentences which they often repeat in some of their favorite magazines to confuse the common people. These middle men are as old as art itself. They are talent less wind bags who surround the talented artists like weeds. They can be found in the court of a king, or near the ministry or the art academy according to the varying forms of social and political systems throughout history. This middle man group makes the life for a true artist almost unbearable. Van Gogh was no exception. The experiments of Van Gogh did not have any value to these art critics. And let us hear some accounts from Van Gogh himself in this context.

….."I can't change the fact that my paintings don't sell. But the time will come when people will recognize that they are worth more than the value of the paints used in the picture."……
….."Your profession is not what brings home your weekly paycheck, your profession is what you're put here on earth to do, with such passion and such intensity that it becomes spiritual in calling."…….
….."In the end we shall have had enough of cynicism, skepticism and humbug, and we shall want to live more musically."…..
……"There is but one Paris and however hard living may be here, and if it became worse and harder even—the French air clears up the brain and does good—a world of good."….

…..."The world concerns me only in so far as I have a certain debt and duty to it, because I have lived in it for thirty years and owe to it to leave behind some souvenir in the shape of drawings and paintings – not done to please any particular movement, but within which a genuine human sentiment is expressed."…..
….."In the fullness of artistic life there is, and remains, and will always come back at times, that homesick longing for the truly ideal life that can never come true."…..
….."Admire as much as you can. Most people do not admire enough."…..

Through his artistic innovations Van Gogh wanted to express "genuine human sentiment" but who will be there to feel that expression? There will be no takers of this "genuine human sentiment" because that does not sell in the market. As I was discussing on the peculiar creature called art critics, Van Gogh might have faced many of them who might have evaluated his paintings and convinced him that those works are even not worth of the value of the paints used to create them. And the man may have faced "enough of cynicism, skepticism and humbug." Van Gogh might have encountered these art parasites in the city of Paris which made him to realize "There is but one Paris and however hard living may be here, and if it became worse and harder even".

Yes it is hard to live with in this culture of naked materialism where money and wealth is venerated as idols and ideals. Where creation, creativity and creator are buried under hanker, lust and greed. Where by building career and identity of a person the person loses the identity of his soul. Van Gogh might have recognized the crudity and vulgarity of this aura and that is why he knew very well that his paintings will not sell as he clearly stated that "I can't change the fact that my paintings don't sell." Yet he knew that "the time will come when people will recognize that they are worth more than the value of the paints used in the picture." He was confident enough. By his deep penetrating insight Van Gogh might have recognized the professionals who were just hungry for the next weekly pay check. He might have been horrified.

As he screams from the core of his heart "Your profession is not what brings home your weekly paycheck, your profession is what you're put here on earth to do, with such passion and such intensity that it becomes spiritual in calling."

Van Gogh might have given the right advice to the wrong audience. The audience had selective deafness. But that did not hindered Van Gogh from resolute persuasion of his own cause.

In deep despair and depression he might have uttered the words "Admire as much as you can. Most people do not admire enough." Yes there in those glamorous lime lights there were enough cynics, skeptics and humbugs but no one was there to listen, observe and admire with an open heart. It was really painful to live in such a situation for an artist like Van Gogh. Yet he absorbed every bit of sufferings day and night. He was going on with his work "not….to please any particular movement" but to express "genuine human sentiment".

Here is a true artistic personality who stands in the history of art just like a mountain and asks the eternal question what the true artists want in life? Wealth! Glory! Fame! Van Gogh himself has given the answer "In the fullness of artistic life there is, and remains, and will always come back at times, that homesick longing for the truly ideal life that can never come true."

True Artists are Embodiment of True Spirituality

I will quote few of Van Gogh's sayings and try to analyze the spirituality hidden inside him.

….."When I have a terrible need of - shall I say the word - religion, then I go out and paint the stars".....
….."I confess I do not know why, but looking at the stars always makes me dream."…..
……"Seek only light and freedom and do not immerse yourself too deeply in the worldly mire"……
….."For my part I know nothing with any certainty, but the sight of the stars makes me want to dream"…….
……"I can very well do without God both in my life and in my painting, but I cannot, suffering as I am, do without something which is greater than I, which is my life, the power to create."…….
……."Love is eternal -- the aspect may change, but not the essence. There is the same difference in a person before and after he is in love as there is in an unlighted lamp and one that is burning. The lamp was there and was a good lamp, but now it is shedding light too, and that is its real function. And love makes one calmer about many things, and that way, one is more fit for one's work."……
……"I feel such a creative force in me: I am convinced that there will be a time when, let us say, I will make something good every day, on a regular basis....I am doing my very best to make every effort because I am longing so much to make beautiful things. But beautiful things mean painstaking work, disappointment, and perseverance."……
……"What preys on my mind is simply this one question: what am I good for, could I not be of service or use in some way?"……
……"In my view, I am often immensely rich, not in money, but (although just now perhaps not all the time) rich because I have found my metier, something I can devote myself to heart and soul and that gives inspiration and meaning to my life."……

…..“If one feels the need of something grand, something infinite, something that makes one feel aware of God, one need not go far to find it. I think that I see something deeper, more infinite, more eternal than the ocean in the expression of the eyes of a little baby when it wakes in the morning and coos or laughs because it sees the sun shining on its cradle.”……

Many times we find Van Gogh is staring at the stars and dreaming like an eternal dreamer. Van Gogh is facing an inner turbulence where he is realizing that there is something more than "I" and that is his "power to create". The man is searching the essence of "something grand, something infinite, something that makes one feel aware of God" and that is nothing but what I call the pure artistic consciousness.

This pure artistic consciousness is the essence of the creativity hidden inside an artist. Rather than going in to the theological reasoning and debates and finding something supernatural and arranging some arguments for the same, an artist like Van Gogh would rather say "When I have a terrible need of - shall I say the word - religion, then I go out and paint the stars". This is spirituality in practice in its purest form. Van Gogh can do well without something supernatural because he finds grandiosity and infinity in nature. From the burning stars in the night sky to the "eyes of a little baby when it wakes in the morning" he finds infinite amount of energy and beauty. If this is not true spirituality then what is? A detailed and in depth analysis of his thoughts will make us realize that the consciousness of Van Gogh was something like unaltered, immutable, steadfast spiritual consciousness of an eternal artist.

In fact Van Gogh was the embodiment of true spirituality. In that same context we have to understand that Van Gogh's opinion on love was just not that of worldly and personalized love. For him love is something which is intangible, yet which is like a fire which can kindle many souls.

For him "Love is eternal -- the aspect may change, but not the essence. There is the same difference in a person before and after he is in love as there is in an unlighted lamp and one that is burning. The lamp was there and was a good lamp, but now it is shedding light too, and that is its real function. And love makes one calmer about many things, and that way, one is more fit for one's work."

Van Gogh's concept of love touches the dimensions of true Platonic love, a kind of love which brings out the potentialities of a person or makes the turbulent heart calm. With this spiritual love Van Gogh looked at things and creatures around him.

Filled with this illimitable love Van Gogh is "longing so much to make beautiful things" and that is why he is feeling a great creative force from inside. Rather than looking at his own interest he is asking himself "What preys on my mind is simply this one question: what am I good for, could I not be of service or use in some way?" That may be the same fundamental question every human being has to face on earth. Almost all persons try to avoid that because they know that this is a very uncomfortable question too. But personality like Van Gogh just goes on searching the answer of the same. Through his life long struggle he discovers his richness even among extreme poverty and says "In my view, I am often immensely rich, not in money, but (although just now perhaps not all the time) rich because I have found my metier, something I can devote myself to heart and soul and that gives inspiration and meaning to my life."

And he finds meaning of life in this way and gives us a direction and a meaning to understand meaning of life. That is more evident and explicit in his following advice to the artists for the future generations "Seek only light and freedom and do not immerse yourself too deeply in the worldly mire".

And that may be the ultimate spiritual message Van Gogh had given to us. A message delivered not only just by his words but by his works and life. While the whole artistic activity of the world is immersing itself in to glory, glamor, grandiosity, pomp and materialistic gains Van Gogh is just standing like a pole star to navigate the ship of art to the correct direction; to the island of love, peace, tranquility and spirituality.

And there in that serene island the artist will seek only light and freedom. Artists like Van Gogh just not only paint on canvases rather their whole life is like a beautiful painting; spiritual and divine. Looking at that and studying that we can learn infinite number of things. That is why I say that true artists are embodiment of true spirituality.

This form of practice of aesthetics can be found very rarely in the history of art and this practice can be termed Pure Spiritual Aesthetics. And what is this pure spiritual aesthetics? That is where the existence of the very artist is for the creation and nothing else.

Plato's Philosopher King and Van Gogh's Pure Spiritual Aesthetics

Let me go little deeper in to the concept of this Pure Spiritual Aesthetics. When Van Gogh says "The only time I feel alive is when I'm painting" most people may take that statement in such a way that as if a painter obsessed to his craft is just venting his uncontrollable emotion. But it appeared completely different to me because I found in this statement what I mean by Pure Spiritual Aesthetics. No wealth, temptation, material yearning, desires can distract an artist permeated with this pure artistic devotion from his duty. It is pure in the purest sense. What is the essence of this devotion?
This is nothing but the essence of true human emotion. Human life filled with sorrow, pain, death, disease, anguish, fear, greed, hunger, jealousy, envy, lust, war, famine is still beautiful because in this small span of life man can create something and that is called art. Man cannot steal anything from this earth. All the things have its natural birth and death. Empires come and go; dynasties disappear, civilizations erode but man can steal few moments from eternity and feel happy and fulfilled when he creates something very beautiful before his eye and show his fellow men that piece of art and say that life is painful but it is still worth living because there is something which is called creation and it makes life meaningful. And when an artist can reach to that pinnacle of artistic realization that time he can say "The only time I feel alive is when I'm painting." The time you are not touching the brush you are dead. This is what is called pure spiritual aesthetics.

The question naturally arises what will be the fate of an artist who takes the path of Van Gogh and strives forward to carry the flame of this pure spiritual aesthetics? The answer is obvious; he will face the same desolation, rejection and ridicule and even resistance from the so called art circles. Nobody in this world have time, perseverance and heart to feel and realize this pure spiritual aesthetics. So the artist will be compelled either to leave painting or to commit suicide.

I often have reflected upon the same and found that this will be the obvious fate of such artists. This problem is an age old riddle in the field of art. After much reflection one idea sparked in to my mind as a solution to this problem.

The only person on earth who can feel and patronize Van Gogh's pure spiritual aesthetics is that Plato's Philosopher King. Why I am landing up in such a seemingly bizarre conclusion? There is justified reason for that. While many artists or art lovers with a tender heart can feel Van Gogh's artistic passion most of them will not be able to patronize him. Because patronization of artist like Van Gogh does not mean to give him some financial support and put his paintings in some gallery; it is far beyond that. And what is that?

As Van Gogh says "To do good work one must eat well, be well housed, have one's fling from time to time, smoke one's pipe, and drink one's coffee in peace". Stricken by poverty and even extreme misery Van Gogh is just asking for least from the society in the material terms. He is just asking to have some coffee to drink in peace. Man like Van Gogh does not bother for his material possession and ask very little from the society in material terms. What he wants is recognition in spiritual terms. And that is appreciation, admiration and adoration and obviously a group of followers who will interact and learn from him as his disciples not only the techniques of painting but they will warm themselves of the fire of his pure spiritual aesthetics. The place where Van Gogh's paintings will be displayed will not be called a gallery but must be termed a place of worship, a conclave of devotion, a cave of mystery, touch stone of passion. Who can ensure that? The rulers!? I do not think that except very few in recorded human history have the intellect and emotion to even address that issue. They have many utilitarian agenda to be fulfilled for their blind folded followers. The only solution is a Philosopher King as described by Plato. Because the philosopher king is essentially a philosopher so he can understand and feel the pure spiritual aesthetics. Philosopher King for better understanding and reflection of the diverse aspects of aesthetics will actually need the passionate creators like Van Gogh.

This sounds utopian; isn't it? I know that at this present structure of society which is just based on some material and utilitarian values it sounds utopian but time will come when earth will be ruled by Philosopher Kings and in their patronage painters like Van Gogh will paint 'Sunflower', 'Potato Eaters' 'Starry Night' and Wheat field under the blazing sun.

"Passion of Vincent" – A New Experimental Painting Media

Let me confess here that while I am greatly moved by the passionate life story of Van Gogh and his profound ideas on art I felt a great void inside me for not taking the path taken by him. For years I wanted to do something in the field of art by which I can offer tribute to this great soul. But I always felt that I am just such a nobody. Can I really do something? Almost twenty years I tried to paint like van Gogh, tried to put paint like him in many ways but all my endeavors ended in failures. I thought it would be so easy to put on colors like him because frankly speaking at first appearance all of Van Gogh's paintings seemed to be very simple and straight forward to me. But I have no hesitation to say that I was deluded by the outward appearance of it. I was engrossed in the techniques and methods. For many years I could not see through and feel the hidden passion in it. I soiled a huge number of canvases in the effort to paint like Van Gogh. Days after days, months after months and years after years I persuaded the same objective only to land up with dirty and soiled canvases rather than to create even a single painting.

Once I came to a conclusion that Van Gogh was having some mental illness and to paint like him one must be mentally ill like him otherwise it is just not possible. I deserted my dream to paint like him. But that was a terrible decision for me because I started to get really depressed and suffer from severe insomnia for almost a year or two.

I thought that I was just haunted by some spirit and somebody was waking me up from deep sleep and telling me that I am nothing but an animated body with a dead soul. And it is really a horrifying experience to live with an animated body which carries a dead soul. By deep introspection I realized that I was just painting like a machine because I was obsessed with the craft. I am painting from my early childhood and it was nothing but a habit or at best to say a hobby for me. Let me confess again that I developed a sense of deep inferiority complex and worthlessness about myself because I was not creative. Even when I was doing outdoor paintings I was just doing it with same techniques and similar tones and shades.

My frustration grew to the extent that I left painting for many days. And there after I felt a 'withdrawal syndrome'. I cannot describe that syndrome logically but it was something like a feeling of deep sadness and negative outlook about each and every aspect of life and situations. I was socially withdrawn and put myself in complete seclusion because I was not feeling good. Insomnia and anxiety were my constant companions for that time. Life was completely dark for me.

I fully realized that to be a perfect painter and to be a creative painter are just two different things. Hundreds of paintings which I have drawn and painted, I thought that they all are just nothing and I am not a painter and I don't know to paint. I just know to put a picture of what I see on a piece of paper or canvas. I am just a nothing and non-entity. Days were indolent and nights were violent. And I started to see terrible dreams and get up several times from the sleep in the night. And those were the nights I started to stare at Van Gogh's paintings hours after hours. I started to read his life story and his quotes on art and life. And frankly speaking I was looking at the paintings with a completely different eye this time. The eye of my mind and my soul. I was in a transformation mode. I was recognizing that a fake artist who was living in my soul is dying slowly. And it was good for me that it died one day. That time I was feeling that I am not a painter; I was just a novice and ignorant creature like a child. I did not know why I started to weep like a child without any reason staring at those paintings of Van Gogh which I have seen more than thousand times. And let me confess I was not weeping like a grown up man I was weeping like a child. I have no hesitation to confess that I wept hundreds of nights and was in complete grief while I was staring at those paintings.

I started to realize the colors, brush strokes and relate them with the heart touching rather heart breaking quote of Van Gogh. I was feeling the soiled hands, smell of linseed, texture of canvases and the sigh of a master whose disciple I always wanted to be. I wanted to touch his hands, carry his canvases, prepare his brushes and stand near his feet to watch him painting. Alas the man is no more. The man died more than a century back. And how did he die? Shooting himself with a gun in utter despair. Then how this dejected, rejected, desolated man's spirit is living with me and taking care of my despair and depression? 'You say Van Gogh died. How dare you say that'? I told to myself. 'Van Gogh is alive and his spirit is living with me in this dark room' I screamed in my mind.

'And his spirit is beckoning me in a lemon yellow wheat field to take up pencil, brush, paper and canvas again and start painting' my inner soul was telling me.

That is how I rediscovered the meaning of Van Gogh - "The Passion", which will unveil itself before you when you are in passion and when you are in need to create. Yes I emphasize the words need to create. This need to create is the first feeling when you really can love arts. And this need is the need to console your tormented soul. The soul immersed in depression, boredom, monotony, darkness, despair really needs light. May be that is why Van Gogh is saying "Seek only light and freedom and do not immerse yourself too deeply in the worldly mire". I just started to have a deep introspection and I was realizing that I was just fettered by different techniques, styles, theories and mediums. It was these very things which were enchaining my mind and I was just a caged parrot who cannot create something emancipated from age old techniques.

And this led me to get determined to do something new to carry forward Van Gogh's fire. I thought that even if I am not capable of then at least to just follow his path. My first conclusion was that to follow Van Gogh's path what I must do at the beginning is that I must not copy his technique. I reminded myself what Van Gogh said regarding this matter "If I cease searching, then, woe is me, I am lost. That is how I look at it - keep going, keep going come what may." In that juncture I decided to start researching to develop a painting media by which we can easily catch light, depict movement, and preserve vibrancy of colors. I found that these were the essence of Van Gogh's painting techniques. That is why I decided to name this new media "Passion of Vincent" at the outset.

I worked with almost all media based on water, oil, acrylic and mixed media but it was not easy to catch hold of all the three qualities at the same time with any single medium. I turned to many media and pigments used by the country side clay sculptors and pigments extracted from vegetables and used by tribal people for their pottery and wood works. But again that was not helping me much although I must say that all of them have contributed to my research and findings in different ways.

After almost eight years of continuous research I can claim that the foundation for this new media has been laid and I have found the basic elements of this media. All the paintings elicited in this book are done with this media called "Passion of Vincent".

I have just not completed my research and I just want to communicate to the world that this is the first version of the media. Many more versions are yet to be developed and that work is still pending. I just want to declare emphatically that this new painting media is not to copy Van Gogh's paintings or his techniques but to go on working to carry forward the fire of Van Gogh. For me experiments in media are more important than perfection because that will ultimately preserve the sanctity and spirituality of art in the long run. In this era of digital technology each and every thing can be reproduced by particular software. In future artificial intelligence will be used for painting and sculpting. While artificial intelligence will reproduce many of the painting techniques, media experiments like "Passion of Vincent" will be a safeguard for the fine arts because digital technology can never reproduce such thing.

Why "The Sadness Will Last Forever?"

When we look at the pre historic art and cave paintings we get just not only fascinated but also we feel sad. This sadness is something which we cannot explain yet we do get emotionally perturbed and get dragged towards those art works. The rock carvings and the paints used in those caves make us extraordinarily imaginative and speculative about the qualities of those human beings who lived and died thousand years back. Although we cannot understand and decipher many of the peculiar symbols and signs still we can feel that a group of extraordinarily passionate individuals are trying to communicate with us. When we stand in such a cave we can feel the presence of the spirit and soul of those artists. May it be the bull of Lubang Jeriji Saléh cave, rhinoceros of the Chauvet cave or bisons of the Altamira cave or hand impressions of Cueva de las Manos, all have the same spirit in common, the spirit of life and spirit of humanity.

Lot of theorists have done extraordinary scientific research on the origin of human creativity but no theory could give us a clear cut answer about what was really the need of this creativity and expression of this creativity. According to my intuitions these prehistoric caves were the early and rudimentary forms of state. The painters of those cave paintings were definitely great philosophers and they were residing in the darkness of caves with their disciples to discuss about life, death, society, roles, authority, art, language, science, duty and so on.

Who knows the peculiar symbols painted in many different caves are nothing but a particular language of communication among them? I think the abstractions, and the symbolic depictions of many creatures on cave paintings were efforts to develop and formulate different theories and strategies for human survival. I further think that the abstract concepts of time, space, cosmology, epistemology, aesthetics and many other deep and difficult concepts of philosophy are hidden inside those paintings. That is why in my mind I always thought that these cave painters were philosophers and their leaders were philosopher kings. When Plato gave us the concept of philosopher king that may not be just a utopia but it might have been a reality in the distant past of humanity which had been forgotten in the din and bustle of civilization.

That is why I am not in favor of those who think that the great philosopher Plato is just giving us some utopian theory of philosopher king and the republic. I just feel pity for those intellectually compromised so called modern day commentators who do not have any intuition, imagination and critical thinking to judge and comment on philosopher like Plato. Plato's theory of universals and forms can definitely help one person to understand the philosophy and aesthetics behind the prehistoric art.

And this is the premise for which I never took cave paintings as just a piece of artwork.

I always have taken it as the places of worship. And that worship was not of a super natural entity but the forces and the things of nature. There was no blindness and blind faith among these old masters. And that was their religion too.

These great masters might have realized very deeply that unless something very beautiful can be displayed before the senses, the raw and wild nature of human being could not be tamed or controlled and all forms of social experiments would come to an end. These masters might have realized that raw human instincts could only be tamed by music, art and particularly fine arts. So the early cave painters were not only painters but they were also philosophers and religious leaders and molders of social mores and principles. They were religious leaders not because they could do some magic or miracles and preach something about extraterrestrial and supernatural or utter some quotations from some selected scriptures but because they could unite people by talking about natural phenomena and reproducing something very beautiful and that was nothing but a piece of art. One may find it very difficult to understand why painting preceded alphabets and symbolic depictions of language. I think that painting is the most important and lucid alphabet for communicating something. Painting is calming and soothing. In other words it absorbs the raw human instincts and aggressions. A calm and peaceful environment must prevail as a precondition to develop further complicated communication system, namely the spoken or written language. So cave paintings were not only early human communication and language but they were unifier also in the social sense of the term. That is why painting can be considered to be the oldest religion of man. And what a beautiful religion was it. Free from any regimentation and blindness. Free from scriptural dogmas and ritualistic dins. It brought people together in a beautiful bond at the same time it preached only one thing that is freedom. Freedom from death, disease, despair and depression.

These early forms of states were not oppressive but they were rather freeing. These states were governed by honest statesmen not by opportunist wealth mongers and their rotten family members. Human creativity originated from this need to create the foundation of the society. Early human states put art and aesthetics above all.

That is why early human pottery and cave paintings depict the sagas of human effort to survive, stories of their companionship and joy and beauty of life. The philosopher kings and their states were to make people happy not by material wealth but by spiritual light. Simple living and high thinking were their motto in life.

I relate Van Gogh's passion with the passion of these philosopher kings because this pristine passion is deathless and it comes back many a times on earth by the life and works of some extraordinarily passionate artistic souls. Essence of this passion is love; impersonal, self-less, unconditional love for creating beautiful things. Free of any bondage, desire and hope to get something material. The same spirit of love we find in Van Gogh when he says "There is nothing more truly artistic than to love people" or "It is good to love many things, for therein lies the true strength, and whosoever loves much performs much, and can accomplish much, and what is done in love is well done".

Now the fundamental question comes what is the true nature of Van Gogh's sadness? Nobody can understand and feel the nature of Van Gogh's sadness without knowing and realizing the passion of the Paleolithic cave painters and evolution of the position of art in the society.

While Van Gogh carries the fire of the pristine passion of the cave painters and the deeper aesthetic values of the philosopher kings the so called civilization ridicules, resists and rejects his ideas, his passion and his fire. So he feels immensely sad and utters "A great fire burns with in me, but no one stops to warm themselves at it and passers – by only see a wisp of smoke". Why? Because the so called civilized people have buried the "genuine human sentiment" under the greed, lust and hanker of creating something very filthy called wealth. And by this wealth they mean only material wealth, money, gold, jewelry.

These so called civilized people have created methods, technologies, scriptures to convert everything around them to something of their own foolish creation and that is nothing but money. And to protect this material wealth they have again created weapons and artilleries. They have frozen heart, ossified brain, calcified soul and putrefied emotions. They are more naked than the prehistoric savage people but they cannot see that because they have intellectual cataract in both eyes and intellectual hearing loss in their both ears. Art is nothing but a piece of product for them to be sold in the market. They don't bother for something called "genuine human sentiment". And that is the essence of Van Gogh's sadness.

For a moment we can presume Van Gogh as a true representative of the passionate Paleolithic painter community and he has just landed on modern, so called civilized world to face the situation prevailing there. What Van Gogh will experience there? He will observe that the oldest religion and oldest philosophical tool by which the "genuine human sentiment" was used to be expressed has now become nothing but the product of a market place. Is it not justified for him to be sad and go in to deep despair? Yes, of course he must be sad.

Artist like Van Gogh does not become sad because he did not get admiration, recognition and place in the elite art gallery. He knew how to fight back and control that negativity. Quite firmly he convinced himself to stand up and fight with the world again as he says "In spite of everything, I shall rise again; I will take up my pencil, which I have forsaken in my great discouragement, and I will go on with my drawing."

So the essence of Van Gogh's sadness is completely different from the worldly sadness which people usually have. This sadness is profound, fathomless and according to me it is divine.

And why it will last forever?

Because this sadness is infinite and it has dispersed as energy on the universe to save the souls of the great Paleolithic masters. It will be there forever and we have to live with it every day every moment and it will haunt us forever.

The "Madness" Will Last Forever

At last I must mention that according to many scholarly articles and essays researchers in the field of history of pre historic art have hypothesized that the cave paintings and the abstract symbols used in those were discovered by Paleolithic shamans. These shamans used to go in a state of trance and see the symbols, figures and the creatures and then after a suitable time they used to paint it. Was it madness? The answer is clearly unknown to me. But I find strikingly similar phenomena in Van Gogh. He says "I confess I do not know why, but looking at the stars always makes me dream." This is the first indication that van Gogh was carrying the same pristine fire as the great Paleolithic painters of human prehistory. And if that is not still enough to prove it then we can discover the same spell or trance in Van Gogh when he says that "I dream my painting and I paint my dream". I cannot explain this trance but I am sure that such kind of spells and trance come to extremely passionate painters where they can see imageries and can reproduce them on canvas. Normal people call it madness but the painter cannot leave this madness because he cannot simply live without it. It takes hold of him and puts him under its influence. This makes him or rather compels him to do creations done never before. The artist at that time cannot take a normal path. Because he knows that normal paths are just barren land.

Van Gogh categorically declares the same in the following statement "Normality is a paved road: It's comfortable to walk, but no flowers grow on it." True artists always choose the path where the flowers grow not the paved roads of monotony and boredom. There is sadness in this path of madness but artists cannot leave this madness. To keep the flame of eternal creativity artists have to choose this madness as Van Gogh said "I shouldn't precisely have chosen madness if there had been any choice, but once such a thing has taken hold of you, you can't very well get out of it."

And this madness will last forever. As long as the humanity is there and there is human soul there on earth will be born artists like Vincent Van Gogh who by their pure artistic passion will vanquish the pride, meanness, vanity and vulgar materialistic lust.

Who will precisely follow the path laid and illuminated by Van Gogh and consciously chose madness to walk on thorny and unpaved paths to make thousand flowers to blossom and break the comfortable paved paths of normality.

Van Gogh said "The sadness will last forever". True. That is never going to end. But absorbing that deep pain inside us we can still transform it into the madness of pure aesthetic spirituality and say that "The Madness will last forever"

"Passion of Vincent" – Paintings

All the paintings depicted in next few pages of this book are done on specially prepared surfaces and done with this new experimental media called Passion of Vincent. This is just the first version of this media. Many more versions are also in the experimental level and will be coming in the future course of time. This version of the media is predominantly based on oil, water and extracts from vegetables.

22 X 14 inch painting done over prepared surface with 'Passion of Vincent'

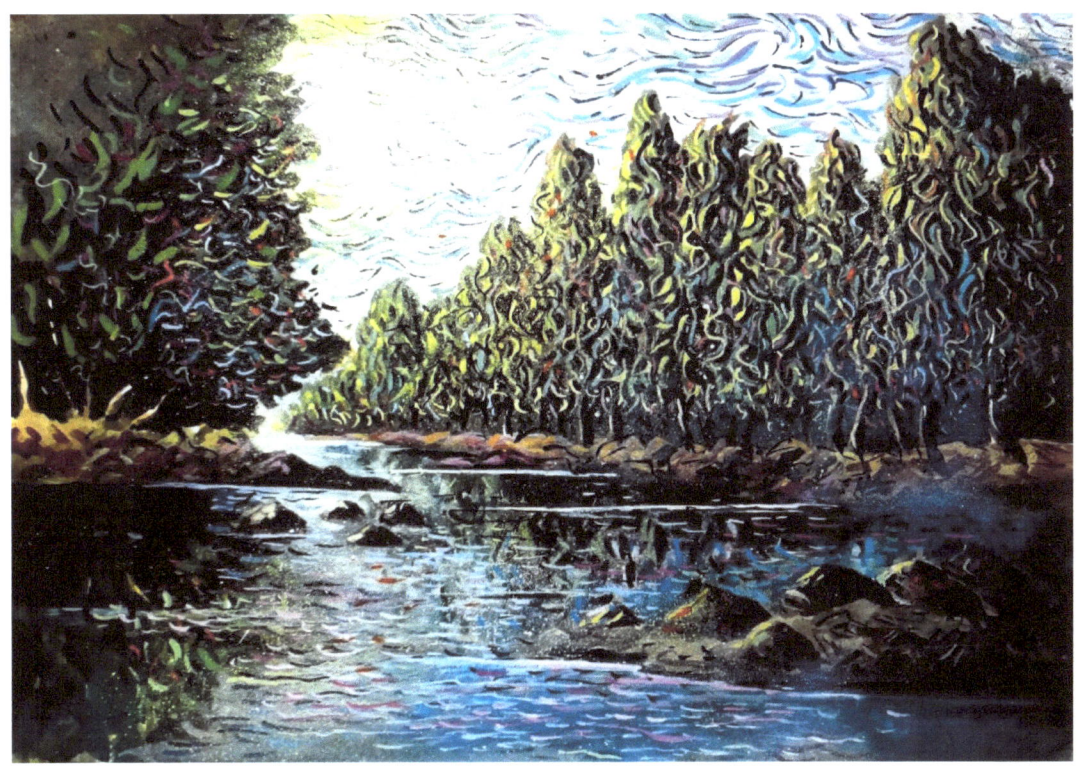

10 X 14 inch painting done over prepared surface with 'Passion of Vincent'

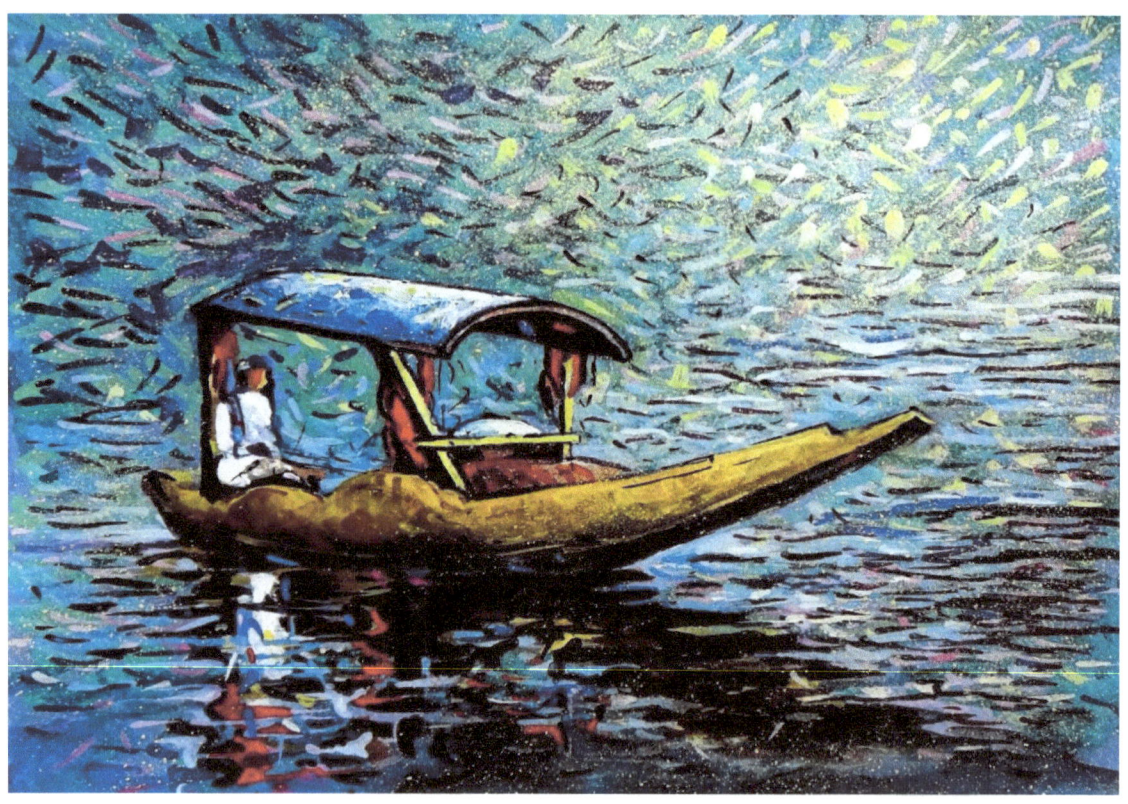

22 X 14 inch painting done over prepared surface with 'Passion of Vincent'

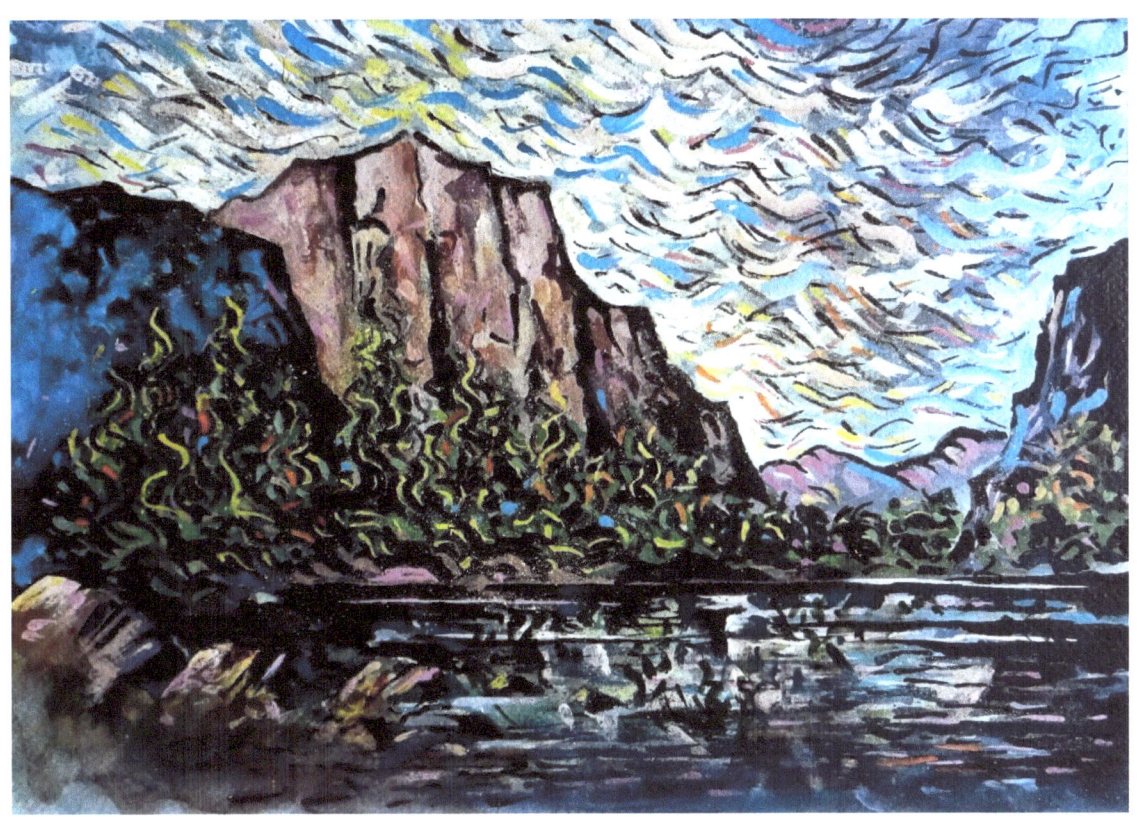

22 X 14 inch painting done over prepared surface with 'Passion of Vincent'

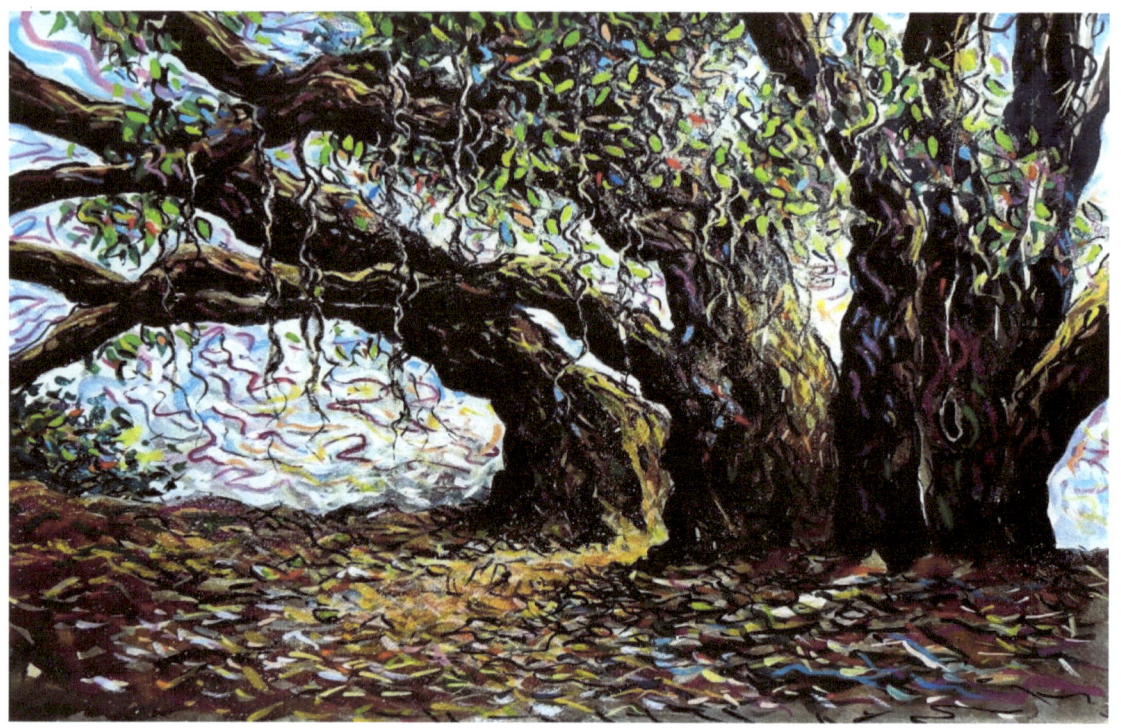

22 X 14 inch painting done over prepared surface with 'Passion of Vincent'

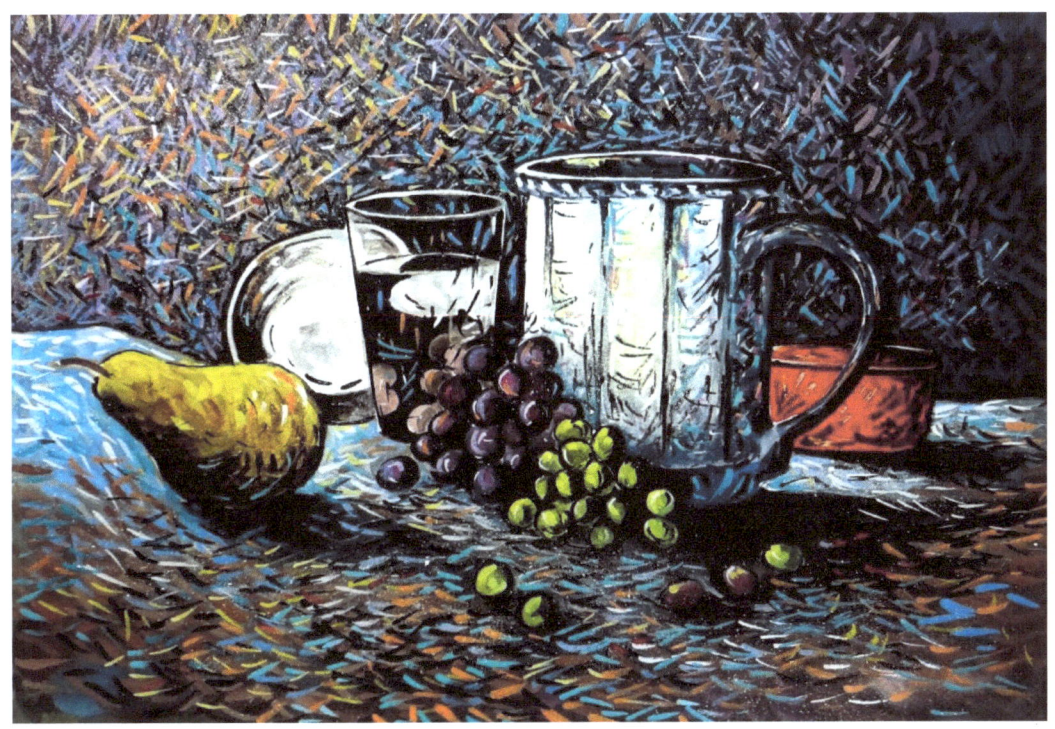

22 X 14 inch painting done over prepared surface with 'Passion of Vincent'

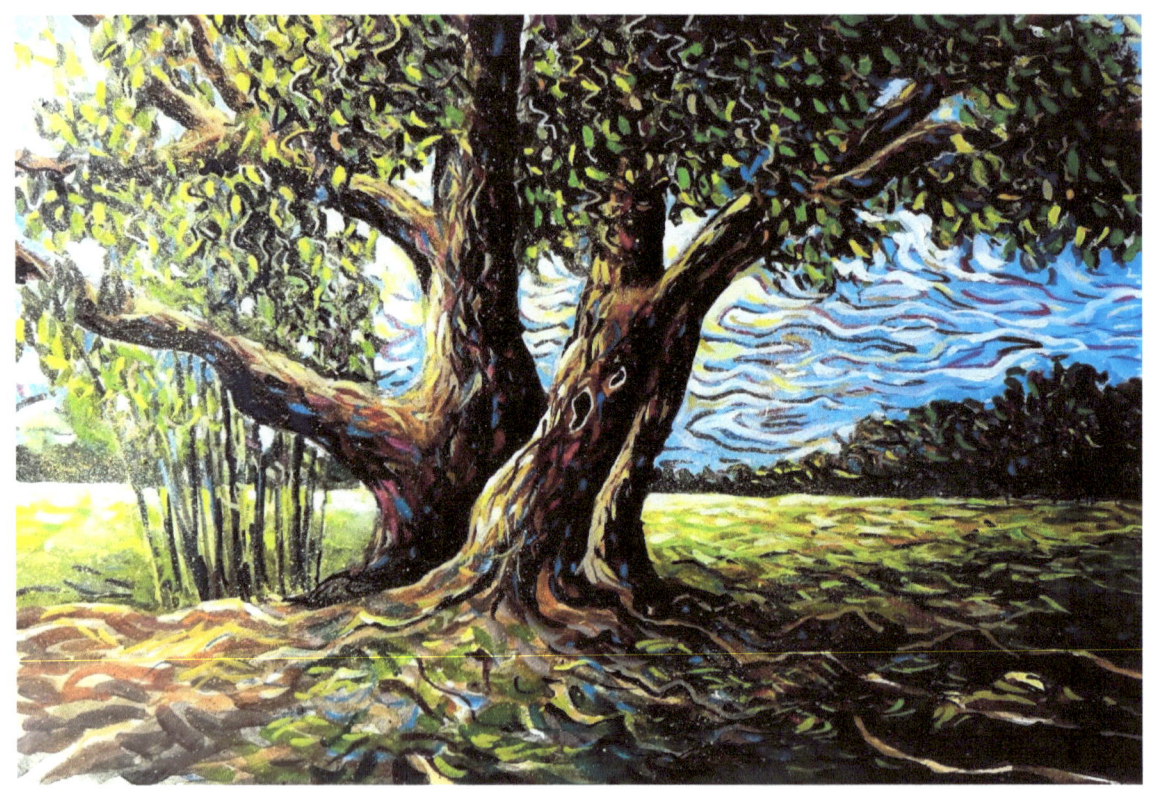

22 X 14 inch painting done over prepared surface with 'Passion of Vincent'

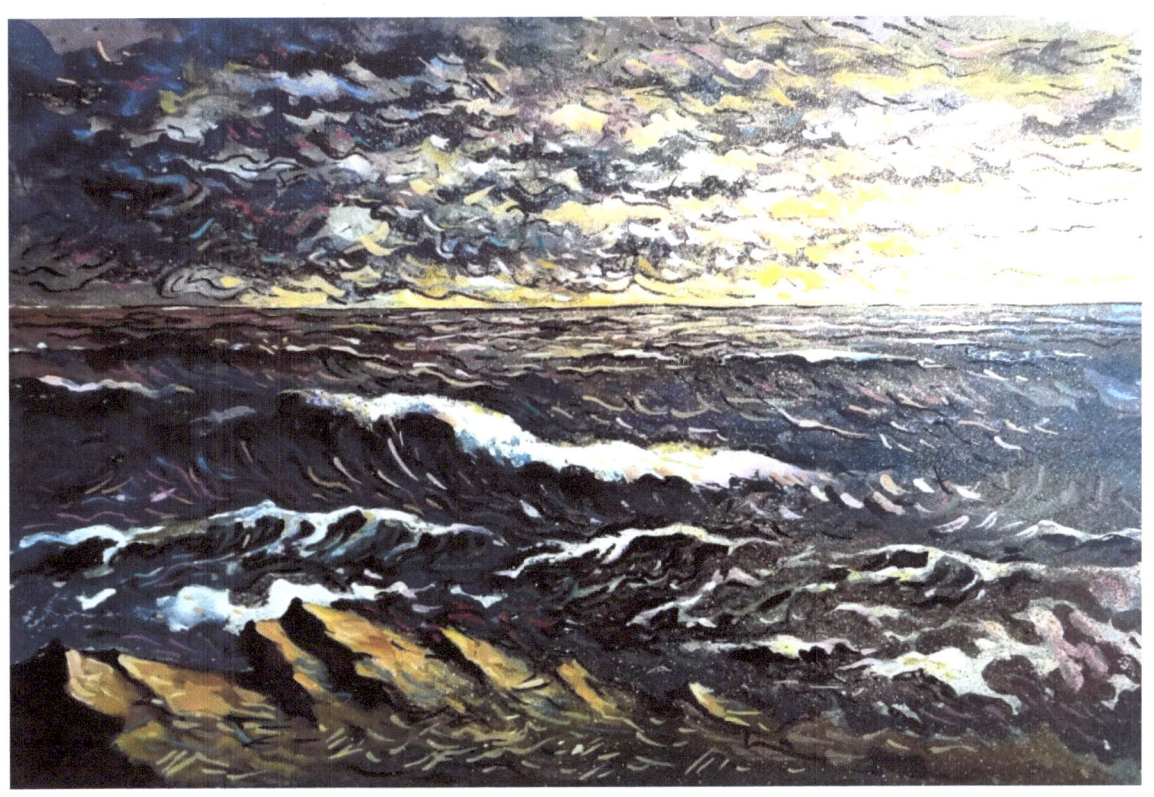

22 X 14 inch painting done over prepared surface with 'Passion of Vincent'

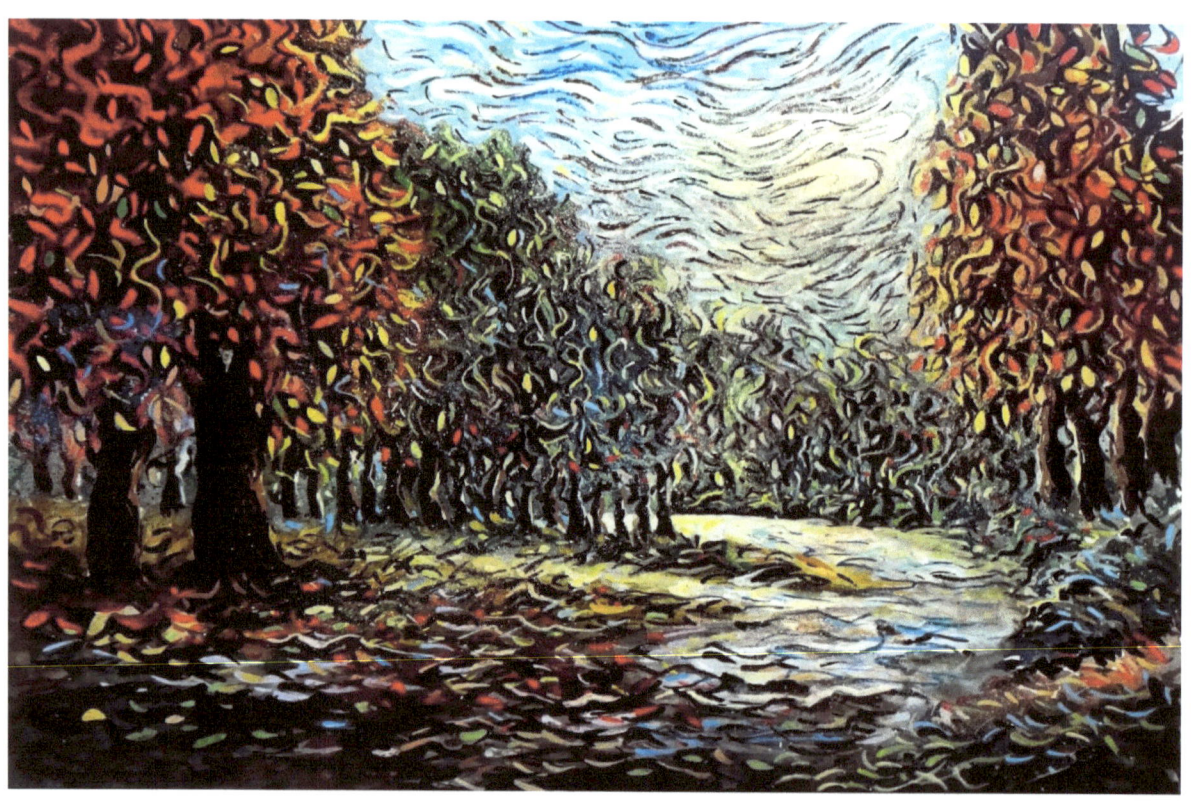

10 X 14 inch painting done over prepared surface with 'Passion of Vincent'

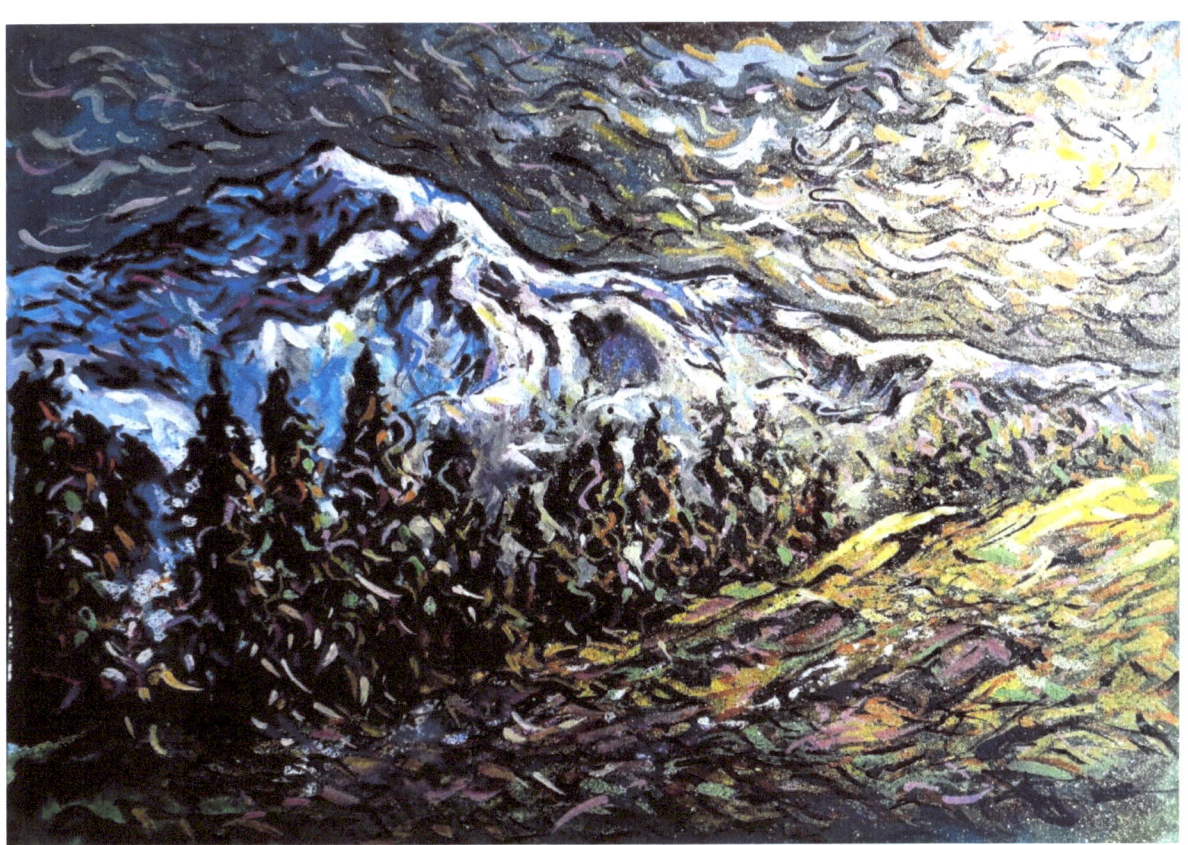

22 X 14 inch painting done over prepared surface with 'Passion of Vincent'

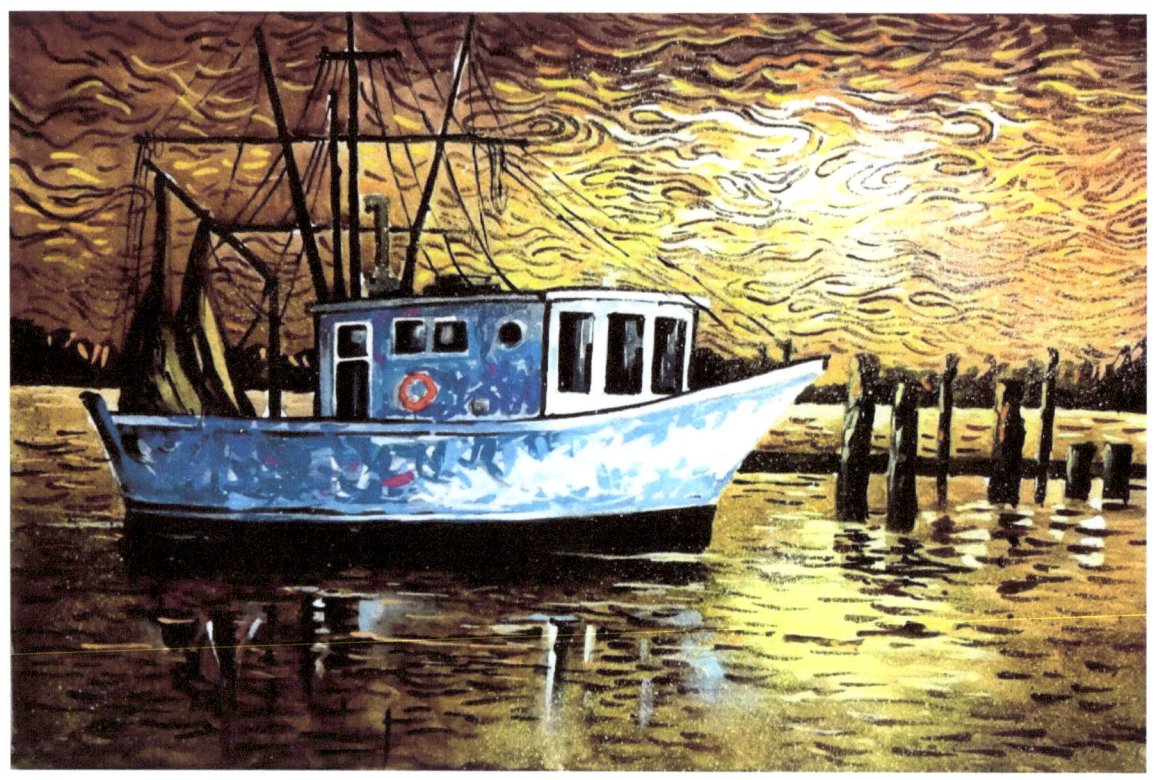

22 X 14 inch painting done over prepared surface with 'Passion of Vincent'

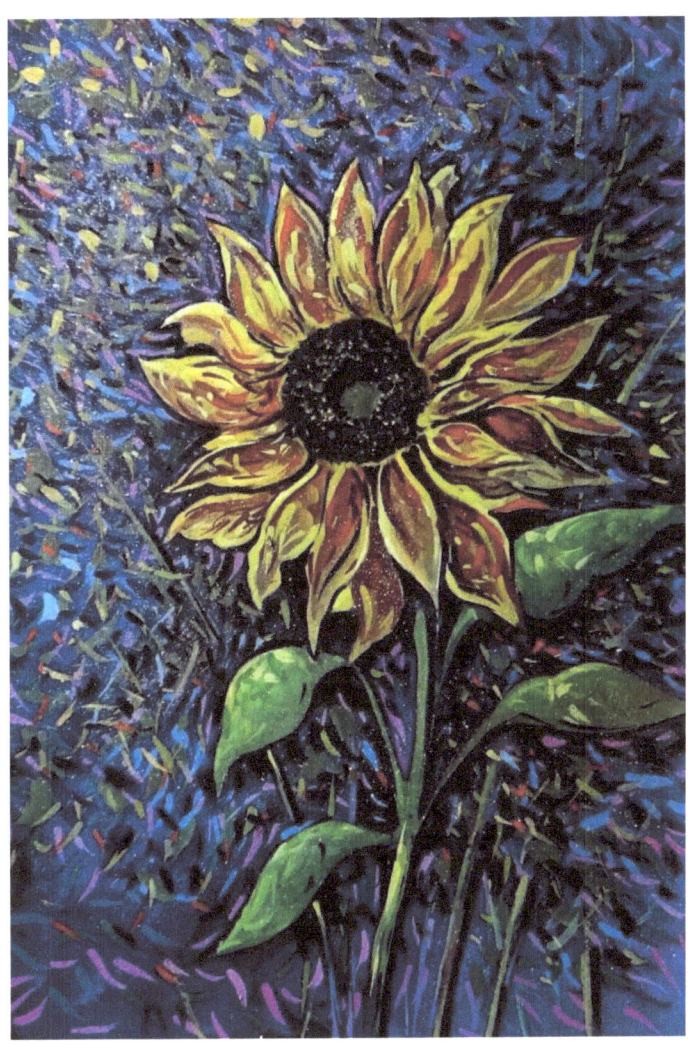

12 X 9 inch painting done over prepared surface with 'Passion of Vincent'

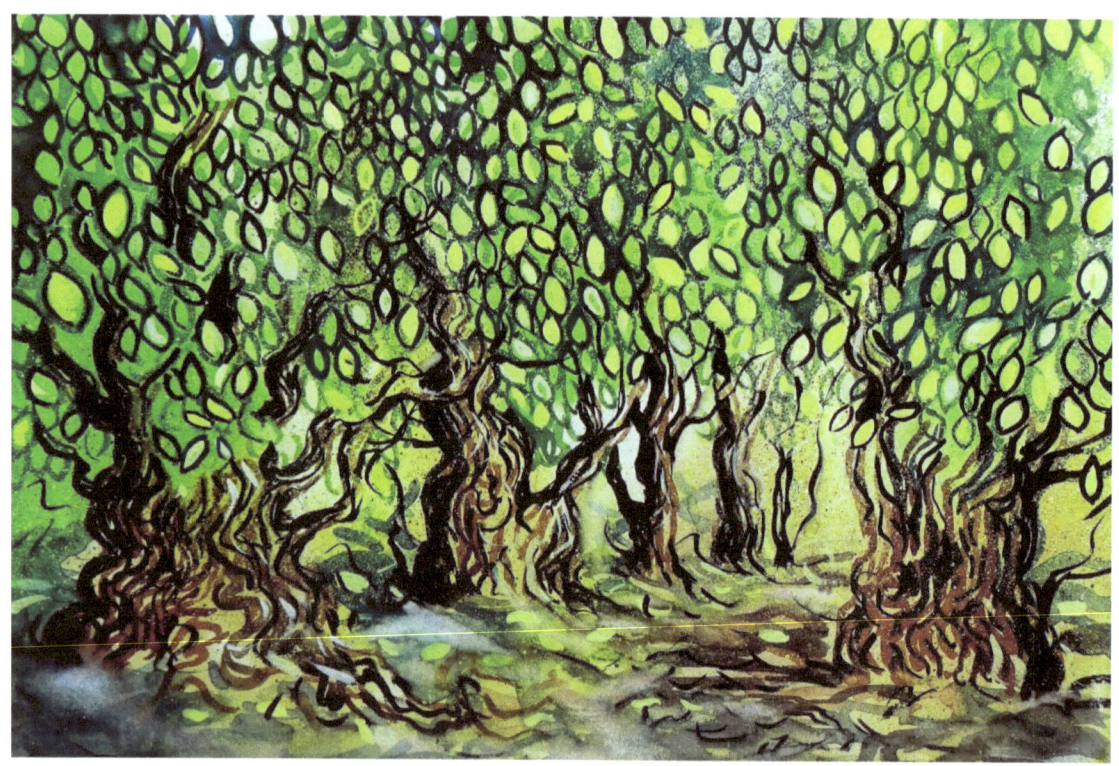

10 X 14 inch painting done over prepared surface with 'Passion of Vincent'

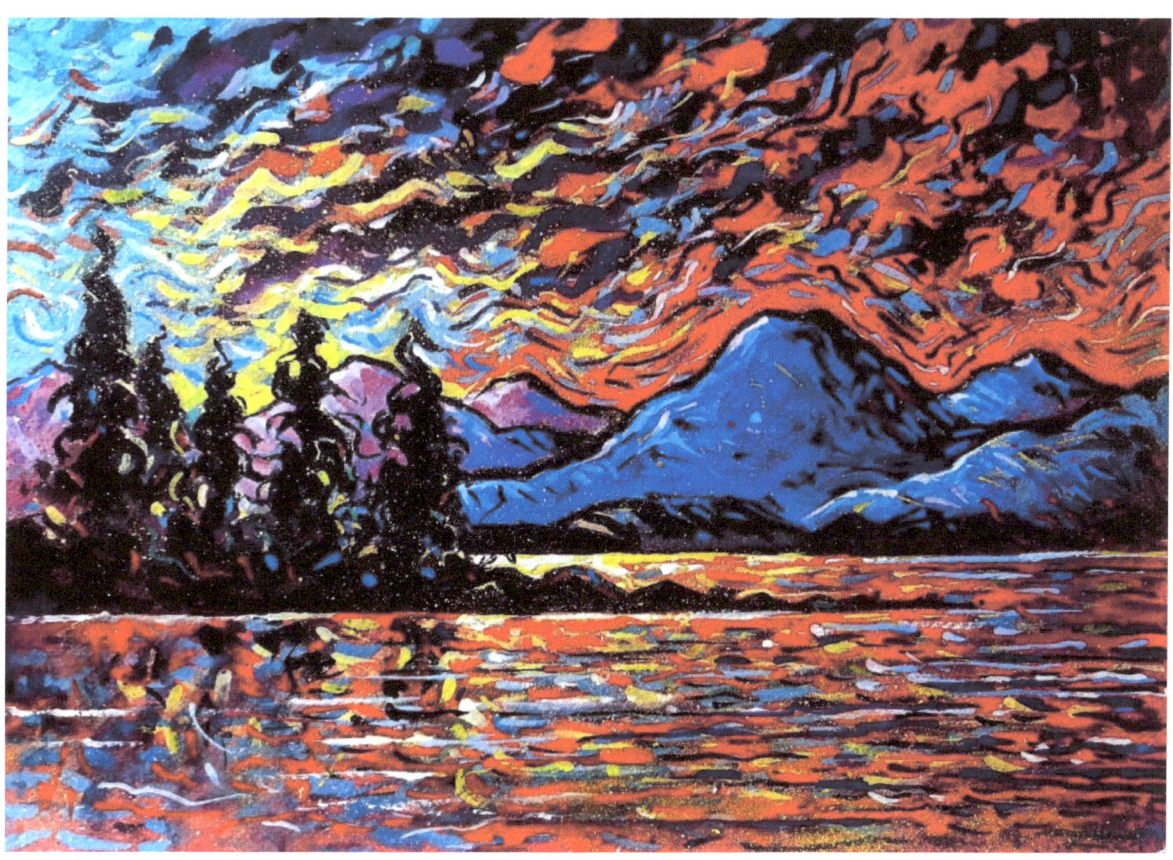

22 X 14 inch painting done over prepared surface with 'Passion of Vincent'

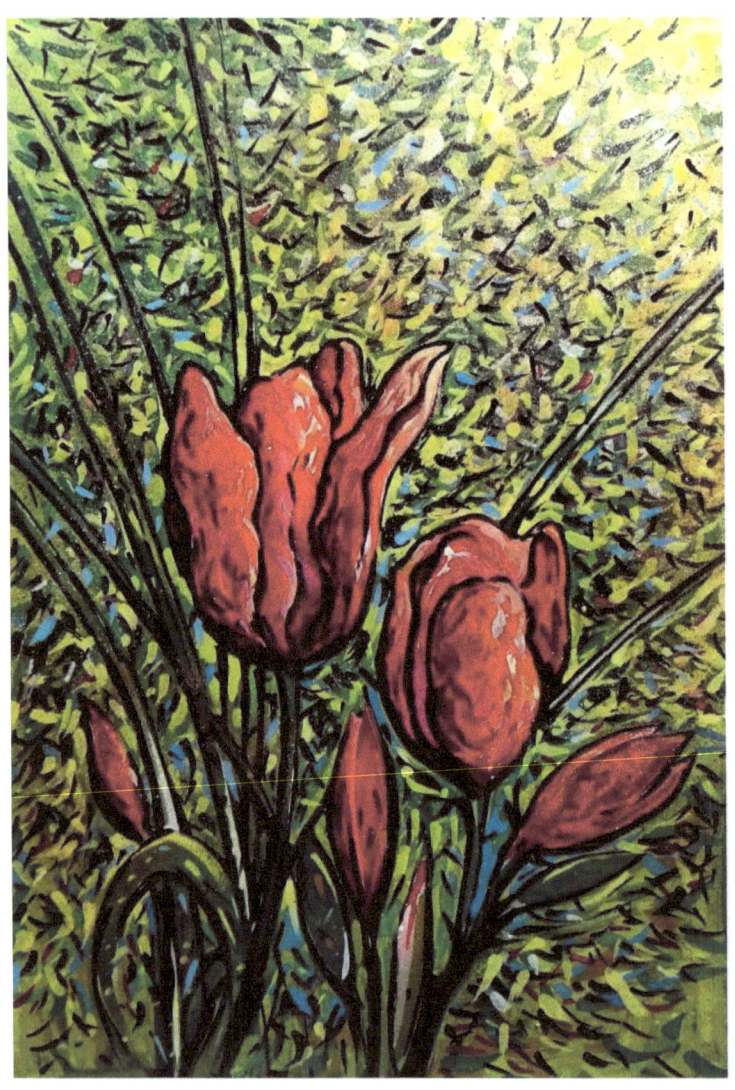

22 X 14 inch painting done over prepared surface with 'Passion of Vincent'

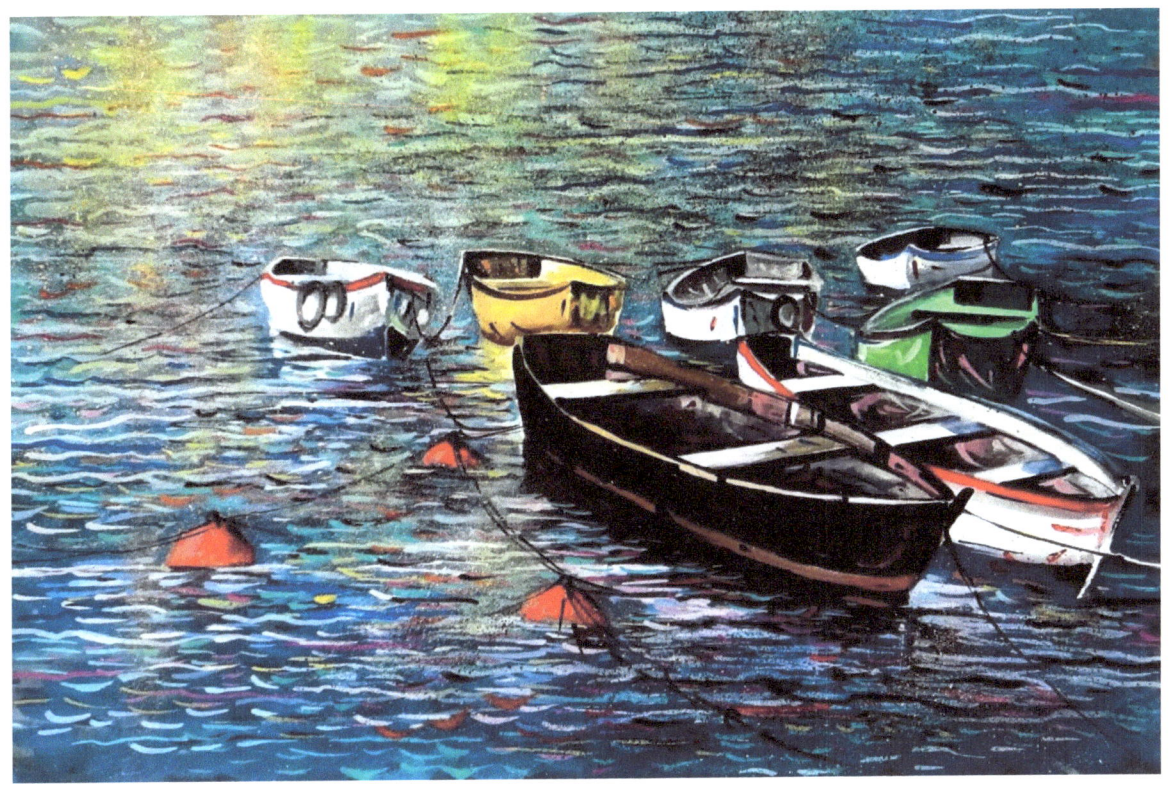

22 X 14 inch painting done over prepared surface with 'Passion of Vincent'

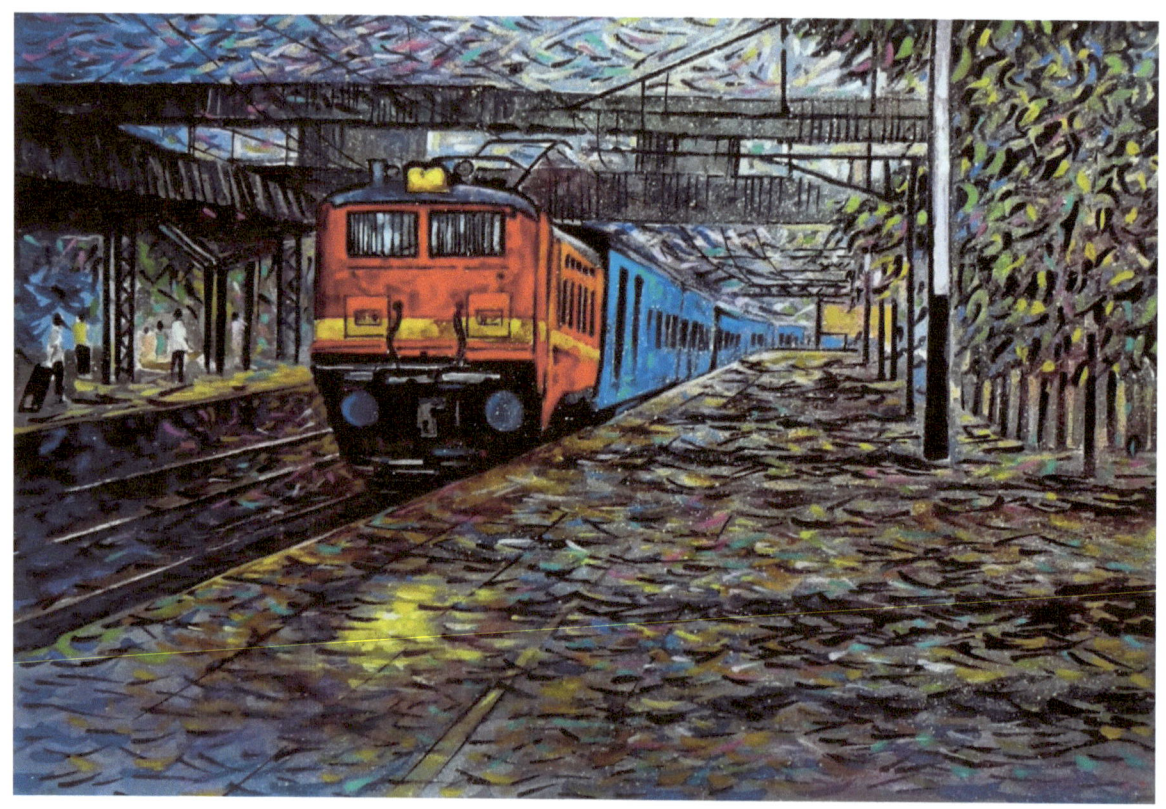

22 X 14 inch painting done over prepared surface with 'Passion of Vincent'

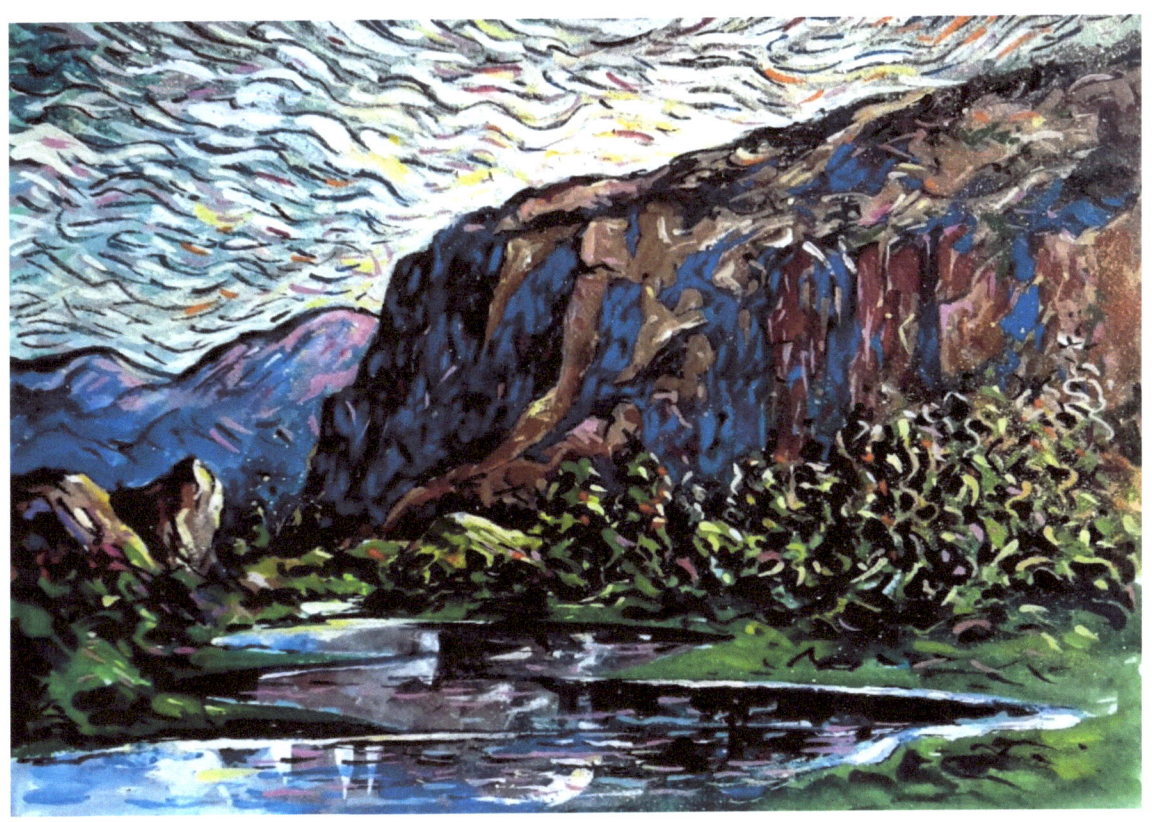

16 X 12 inch painting done over prepared surface with 'Passion of Vincent'

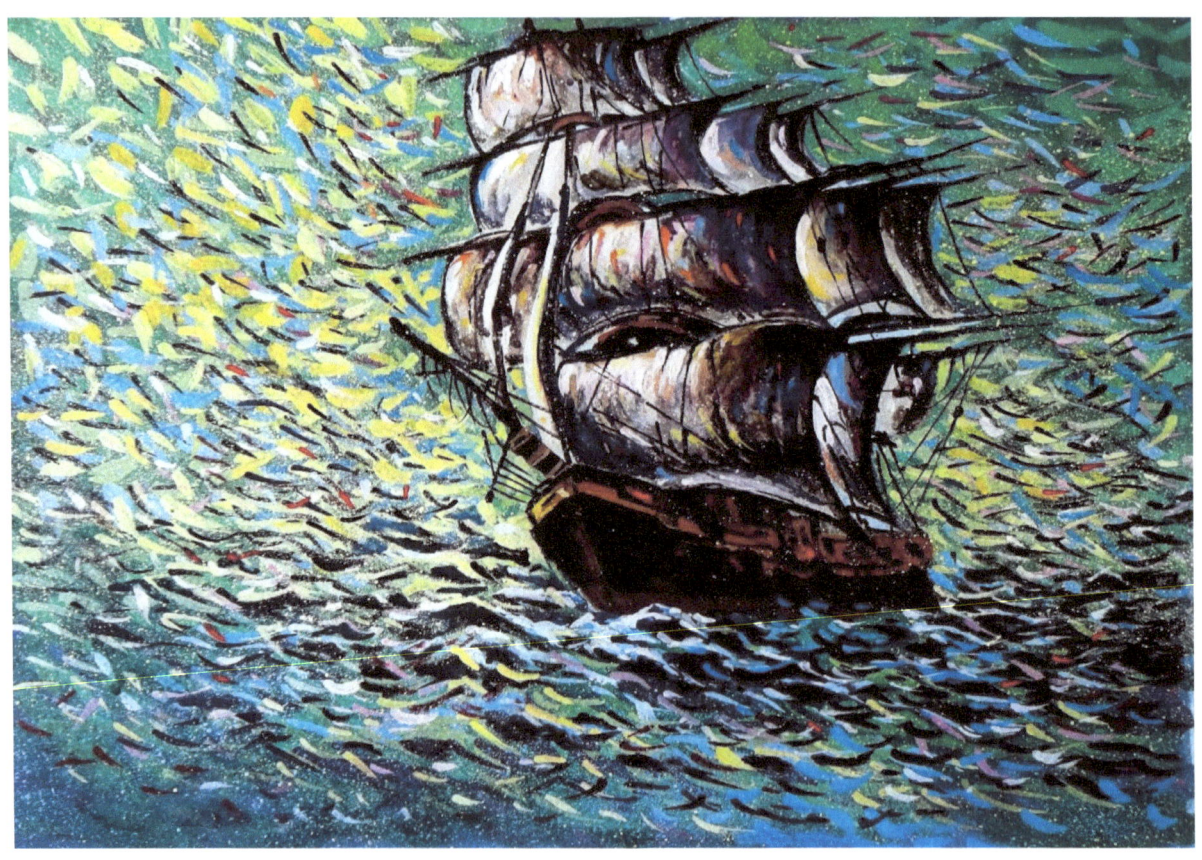

22 X 14 inch painting done over prepared surface with 'Passion of Vincent'

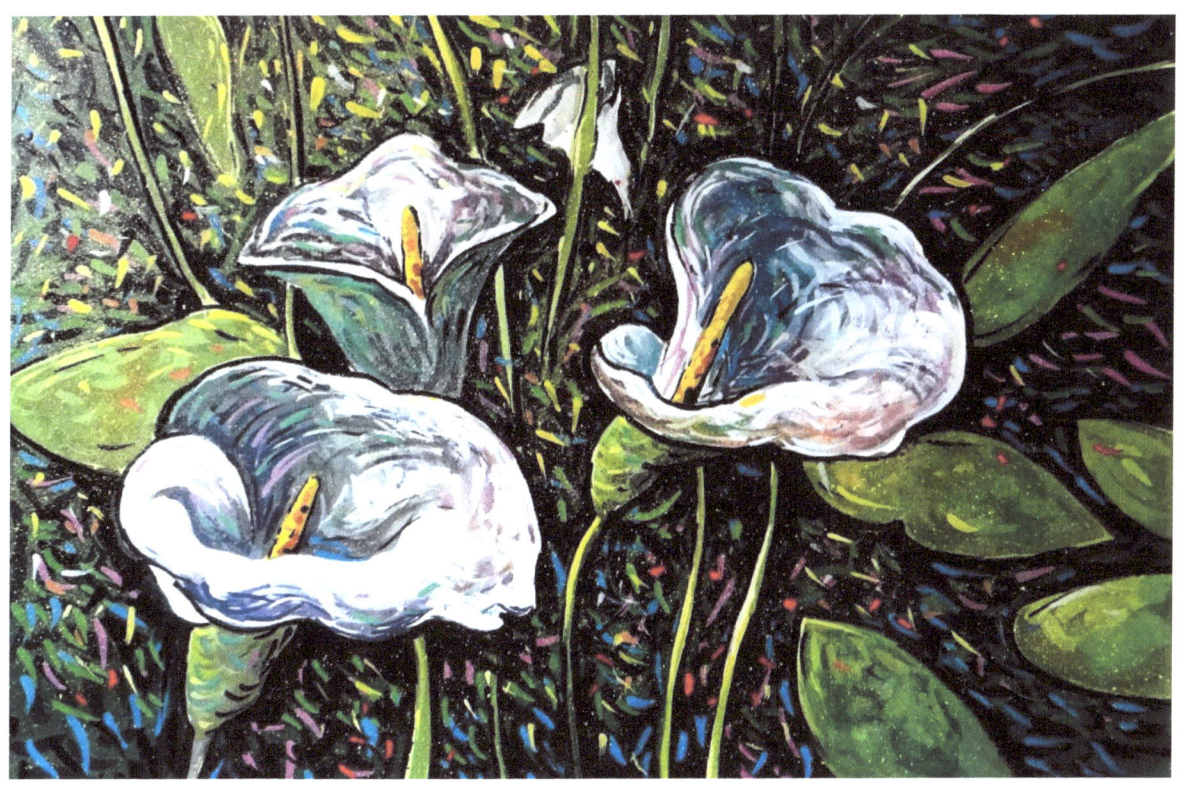

22 X 14 inch painting done over prepared surface with 'Passion of Vincent'

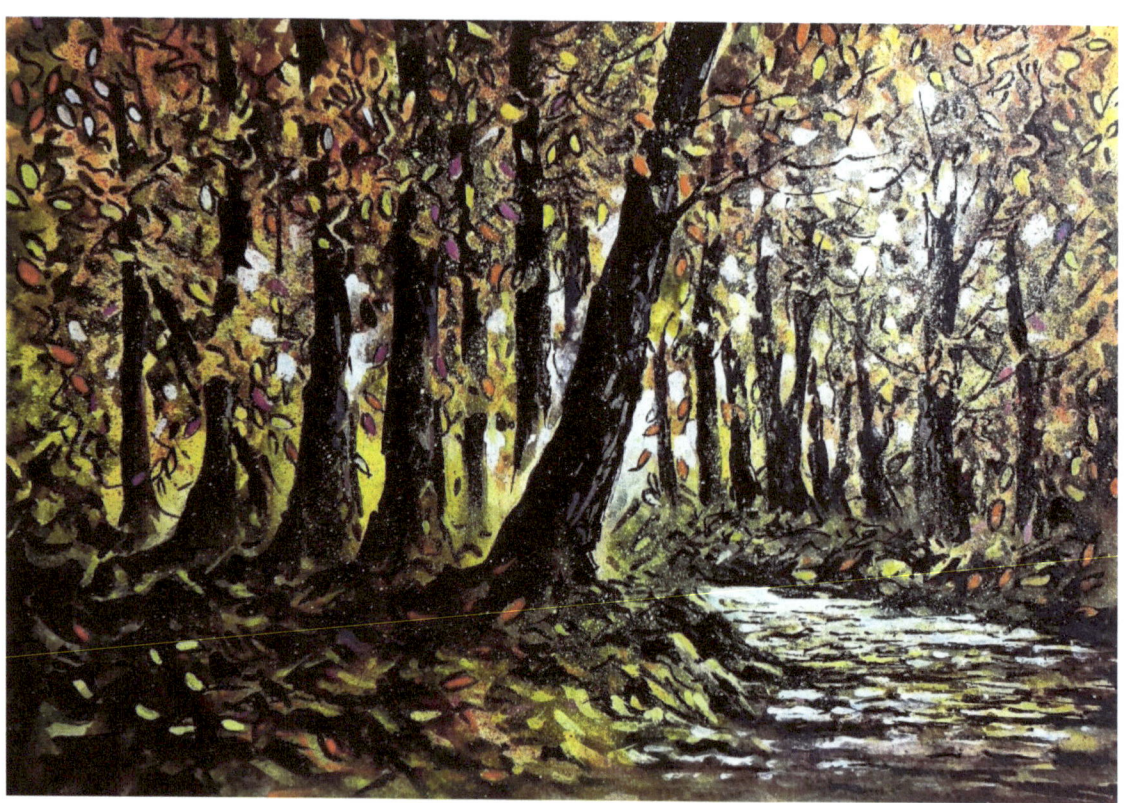

10 X 14 inch painting done over prepared surface with 'Passion of Vincent'

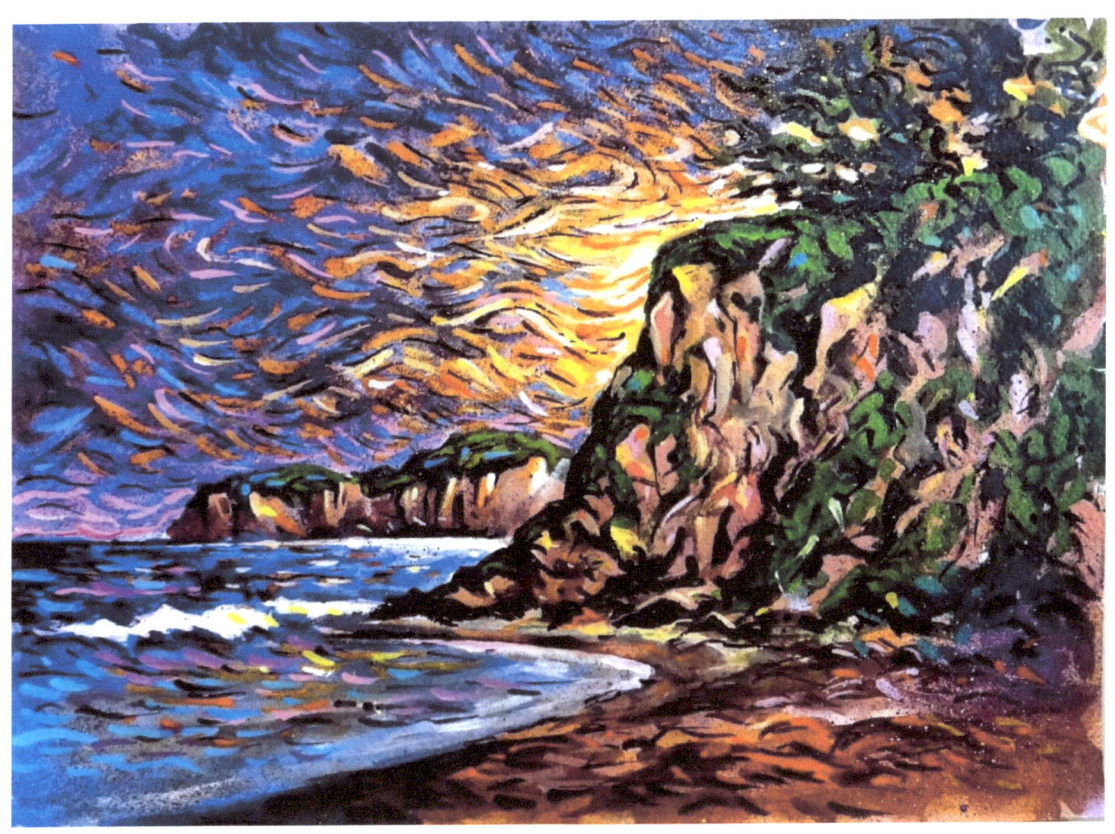

22 X 14 inch painting done over prepared surface with 'Passion of Vincent'

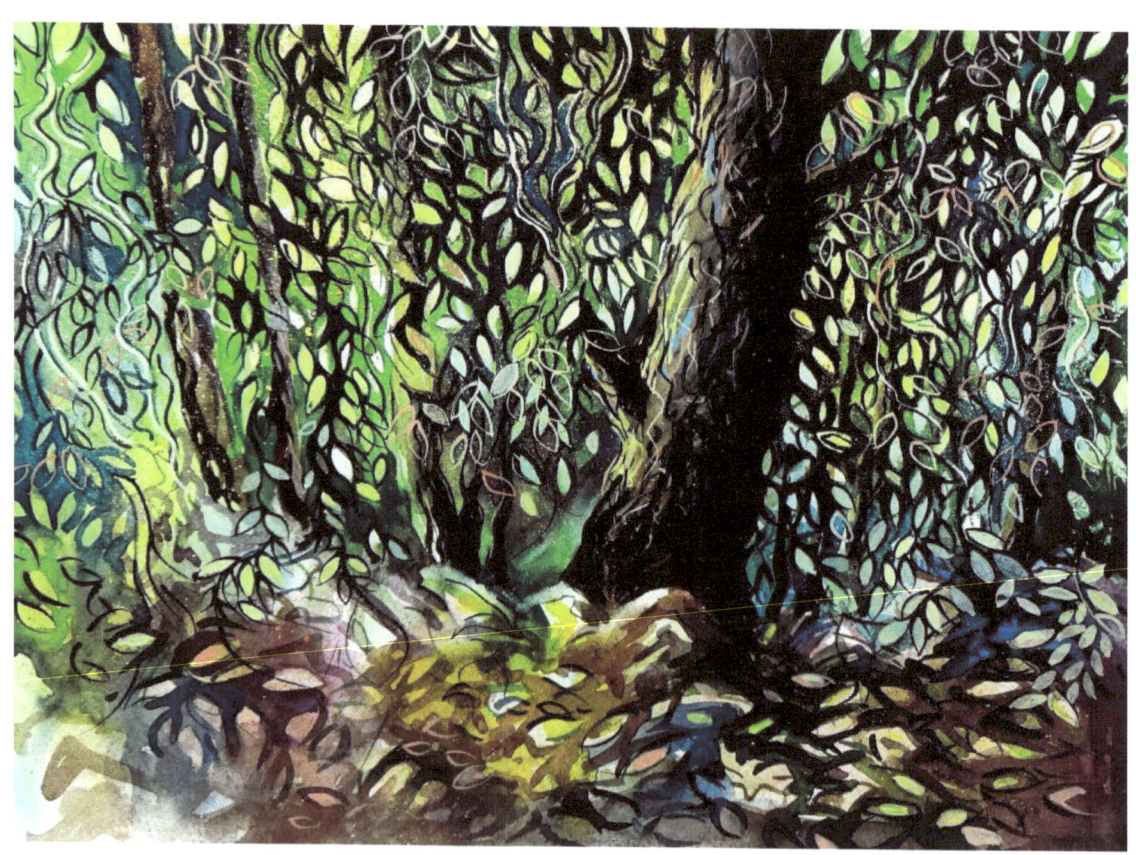

10 X 14 inch painting done over prepared surface with 'Passion of Vincent'

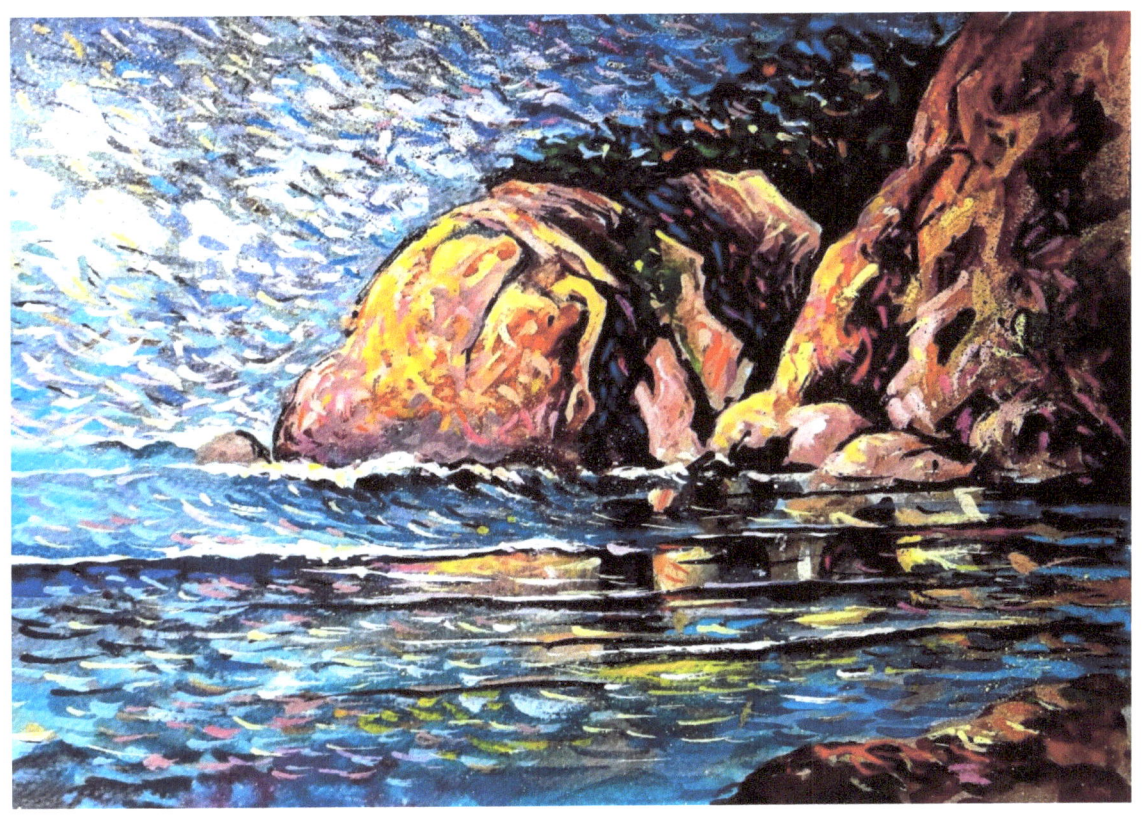

10 X 14 inch painting done over prepared surface with 'Passion of Vincent'

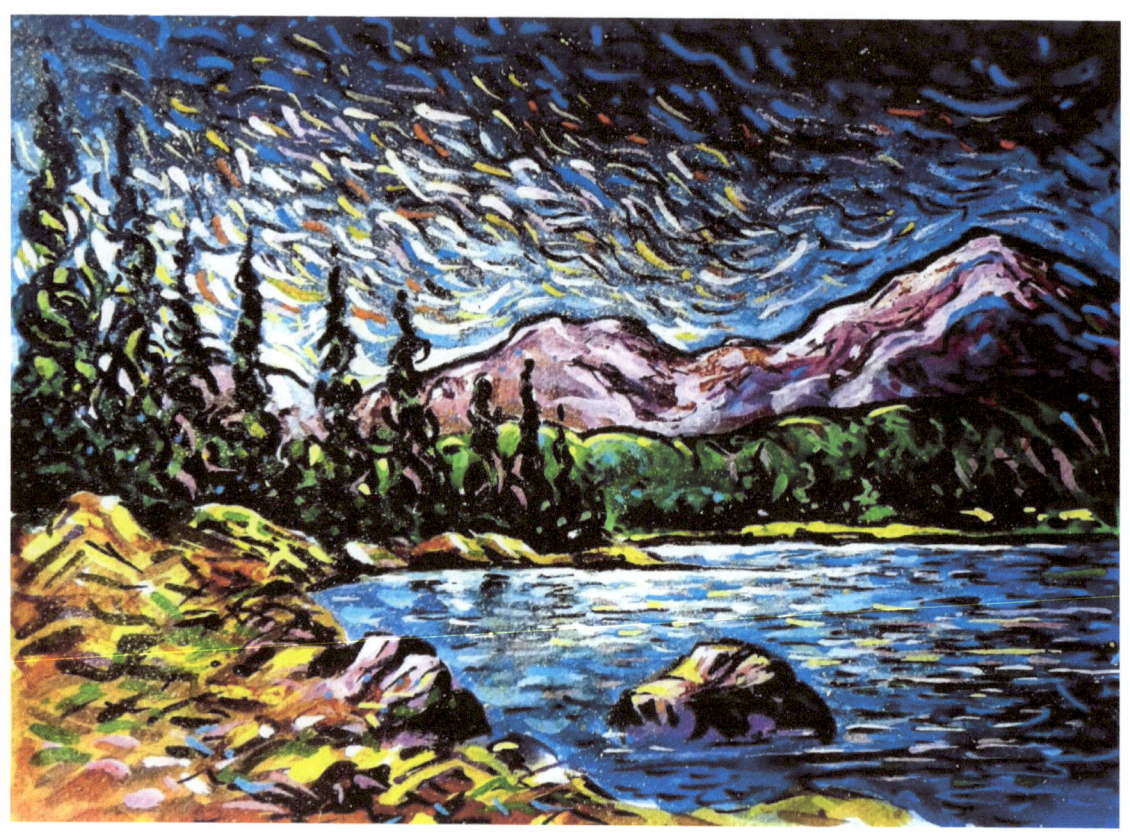

10 X 14 inch painting done over prepared surface with 'Passion of Vincent'

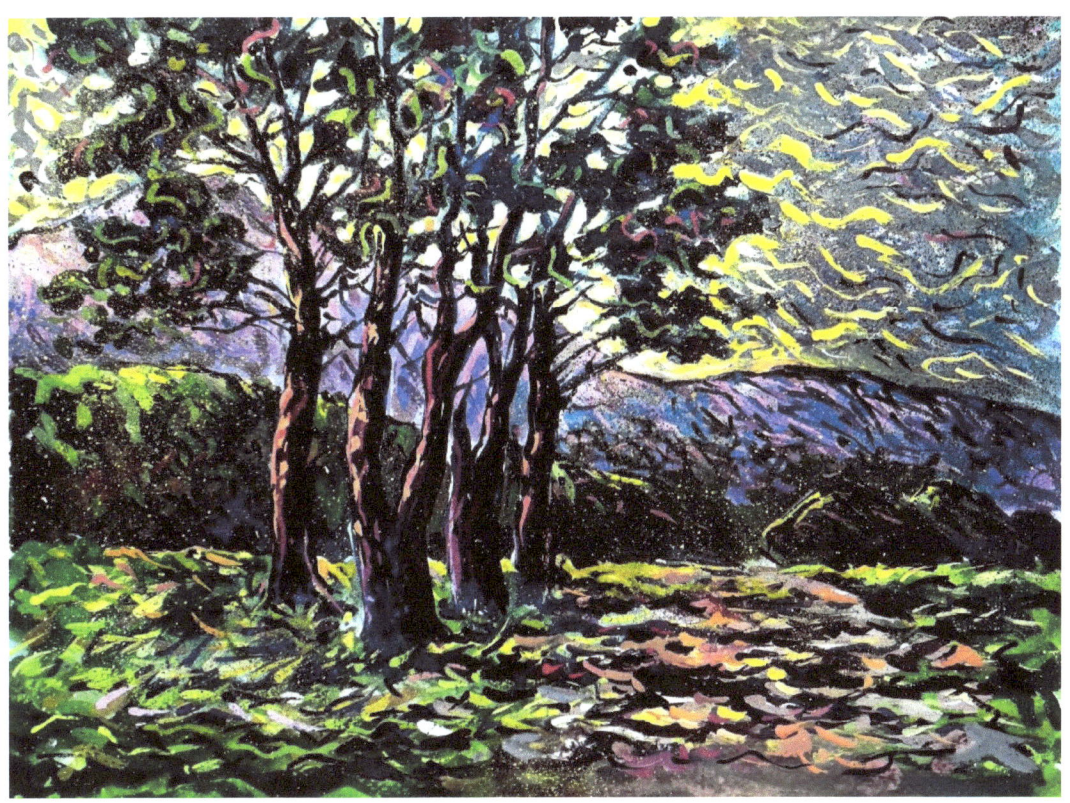

www.ingramcontent.com/pod-product-compliance
Lightning Source LLC
Chambersburg PA
CBHW051204220526
45473CB00003B/897